FASCINATING CITIES
ROME

The Swiss Guard – the Pope's bodyguard – has a history stretching back over 500 years. Here, newly sworn-in guards take part in a mass in St Peter's Basilica.

The Piazza della Rotonda, named after the Pantheon, is one of the most beautiful and atmospheric squares in the city: a setting for romance, and a meeting point for young and old, by day and night.

ABOUT THIS BOOK

Some 3,000 years ago, Rome's first settlers occupied a bend in the Tiber, the heart of today's Rome. Traces of them still remain, which is why Rome attracts those who are interested in history and culture. Walking through the Eternal City, the presence of its mythical founder, King Romulus, is felt as strongly as that of the great emperors of ancient Rome, when the city governed much of the world, or the popes who ruled the city in Renaissance and baroque times. In Rome, as in no other city, you can see the roots of Western civilization.

But Rome is not a museum. In the shadow of millennia-old monuments, life is lived in an infectious, truly vital way. The city's restaurants, bars, markets, streets, and squares are filled with the bustle of business. The atmosphere is lively and stimulating, the Roman temperament echoing the hectic pace of Latin life, but life in Rome does not always have to be lived in the fast lane. As Goethe said: "Here the current takes you away as soon as you step into the boat".

One of the chief destinations on the Grand Tour for wealthy Europeans in the 18th and 19th centuries, Rome now attracts millions of visitors every year – as Robert Browning said: "Every one soon or late comes round by Rome."

This book is intended above all to encourage readers to make their own discoveries. An overview of the history of the city, and of the empire to which it gave its name, is followed by chapters full of photographs and information on the historic city center, the remaining ancient buildings, and the Vatican, as well as on places of particular interest in other suburbs and the area around Rome. We hope that these, combined with the final map section and the web addresses included in the comprehensive index, will allow readers to discover as much as possible for themselves.

Wolfgang Lamuth

The city, the river, and the dome of St Peter's. At night the shadows of the past seem to rise up from the waters of the Tiber and hover peacefully over the roofs of the Eternal City.

"My Rome? – Not even Nero allowed himself to speak of 'his' Rome," said the journalist Franca Magnani, a Roman by birth. This might well be due to the fact that a city that has for so long been an object of desire for so many people from all over the world cannot possibly belong to just one person. So on the one hand, Rome belongs to no one – not the Romans, because they have to share their treasures with awestruck tourists, and not the tourists, because they are only here as guests. On the other hand, Rome belongs to all who enter this city and understand it, as did Federico Fellini when he said, "Rome is a carousel of memories, real events, and dreams. All the embellishments one could require for a lifetime's films are combined here."

CONTENTS

Rome, city of angels: the Castel Sant'Angelo was originally built as a mausoleum for the emperor Hadrian (76–138, emperor from 117), who also built the bridge over the Tiber here in 134.

Emperor Trajan (53–117, emperor from 98) constructed one of the largest and now best-preserved of the imperial forums. The Roman Empire reached its greatest geographical extent under Trajan's rule.

TIMELINE

Napoleon once remarked that the history of Rome was also the history of Western civilization. If you follow the development of the city from its beginnings in about 1000 BC to the present day, you will have an overview of the development of European culture, but you will see that it did not always follow an upward curve. On its path from its origins as the glorious heart of a global empire, through the seat of Christianity to the capital of Italy, Rome, the Eternal City, had to overcome many setbacks before returning to its former brilliance.

The poets Virgil and Livy were convinced that the Romans had been *princeps terrarum populi*, the first people on earth. Many painters, especially during the Renaissance, took their themes from the myths of the city's foundation.

Right: *Aeneas' Flight from Troy* (Federico Barocci, 1598); *The Apotheosis of Aeneas* (Pietro da Cortona, 1651); *Mars and Rhea Silvia* (Peter Paul Rubens, circa 1616).

The mythical past
According to legend, after a long war the city of Troy was conquered by the Greeks, using the Trojan Horse.

...
Under the leadership of the hero Aeneas, fleeing Trojans land in Italy.

...
Aeneas marries the daughter of a local ruler and founds a city.

...
Aeneas' son Ascanius founds the city of Alba Longa, to the south of contemporary Rome.

...
Numitor, the king of Alba Longa, is overthrown by his brother Amulius.

...
Rhea Silvia, the daughter of Numitor, is forced into a life of celibacy as a priestess.

Gods and heroes

In the 3rd century BC, when Rome proudly called itself *caput mundi*, the capital of the world, the legend of the foundation of this powerful city was well known. In his epic poem the *Aeneid*, Virgil (70–19 BC) told the story of Aeneas – the son of a king and the goddess Aphrodite – who defended the city of Troy for a long time against the attacking Greeks. According to the poet, when the Greek hero Odysseus finally managed to break the resistance of the defenders, Aeneas and his son fled with a small trusty band of followers.

After a long voyage, the group was driven onto the coast of Italy, where Aeneas married Lavinia, the daughter of a local leader. Their son Ascanius founded the city of Alba Longa in the hills to the south of today's Rome. It became the "mother city" of Rome, and was the birthplace of a legendary pair of twins ...

Romulus and Remus

When Numitor, king of Alba Longa, was overthrown by his brother Amulius, the usurper forced Numitor's daughter to become a priestess in the temple of Vesta. As a vestal virgin, she

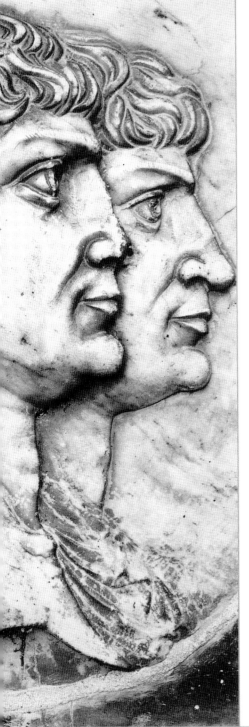

The twins Romulus (left in picture) and Remus, mythical founders of Rome, portrayed in a marble relief from imperial Rome.

was pledged to chastity, so under "normal" conditions would not be able to bear any descendants, who could later challenge Amulius for the throne. But the god of war, Mars, was so incensed by the brazen usurper that he forced his way into the temple of Vesta and made Rhea Silvia pregnant. When she gave birth to twin sons, Amulius commanded that the boys be drowned in the Tiber. But the boat-shaped cradle in which Romulus and Remus were launched was washed up on the shore. A she-wolf looked after the babies, protecting and suckling them until they were discovered by a shepherd, who then brought them up. When the twins came of age, they killed the usurper and

restored their grandfather to power. The Roman historian Livy (59 BC–AD 17) wrote

The mythical past to 1000 BC
Legendary beginnings

...
Rhea Silvia gives birth to the twins Romulus and Remus, whose father is said to be Mars, the Roman god of war.

...
The usurper Amulius abandons the twin boys on the banks of the Tiber.

...
A she-wolf saves the children from death by protecting and suckling them.

...
Amulius is overthrown by Romulus and Remus, as the grandsons of the rightful ruler.

...
Romulus kills his brother in a fight; he founds the city named after himself on the Palatine Hill.

Around 1000 BC
Evidence of an Iron Age hut settlement dating from this time has been found on the Palatine Hill.

Left: The Capitoline she-wolf suckles Romulus and Remus – for a long time this sculpture was believed to date from the Etruscan era.

Left: The eternal myth of the foundation of Rome: Romulus and Remus abandoned on the banks of the Tiber, in a contemporary setting (engraving by Matthäus Merian the Elder, 1630).

that the twin brothers wanted to found a city at the place where they had been abandoned. Romulus made his way to a hill, now called the Palatine Hill; Remus went to another, now called the Aventine. Whichever one of them saw the most birds in flight, they agreed, would be the victor in the contest between the two rival brothers to see who would rule the newly founded city.

Remus saw six vultures, and a little later Romulus saw 12. This had fatal consequences for the loser, who could not accept his defeat that easily. Livy gave two versions of what happened next: in one version, there was a violent fight, in which Remus was "knocked down in the tumult". According to the other, better-known, version, Remus apparently jumped mockingly over his brother's new walls and was then killed by the incensed Romulus, with the words: "This is what will happen in future to anyone who jumps over the walls of the city!"

The mysterious she-wolf

It seems reasonable to doubt the historical accuracy of the *fama*, as Livy calls the legend in the Latin original. Livy thought it was possible that the mother of the twins had been raped but felt it was more "noble" to claim that Mars was the father of her children. In addition, many believed that the wife of the shepherd was called "she-wolf" because she gave her body without discrimination. Livy took this to be the real "origin of the wonderful legend".

Whatever scraps of truth may lie behind the legend of Rome's beginnings, the city went on to become one of the founding cities of Western civilization and was also to play a significant role in the long history of Christianity.

Poetry and truth

Archeological excavations have shown that there were hut settlements on several of Rome's "seven hills" in the Iron Age. The oldest was on the Palatine Hill. It is possible that in around 753 BC – the year to which Livy dates the foundation of the city – the individual settlements joined together into a community. The hills were not high, but here, at the intersection of ancient trade routes, mainly transporting salt, they were strategically significant. At the point where the city gradually grew up, the island in the Tiber now known as the Isola Tiberina formed a useful crossing

Model of an Iron Age hut on the Palatine Hill.

point over the river. The island has its own legend, which says that Rome's citizens threw the body of the tyrant Tarquinius Superbus into the river, where silt gradually accumulated around it until it became an island. But the raw facts cannot compare to the more vibrant myths. Perhaps it's best to go along with a common Italian saying: "*Se non è vero, è ben trovato*" – "If it's not true, at least it's a good story".

Right: Numa Pompilius, the second king of Rome, with his lover, the nymph Egeria (painting by Angelica Kaufmann, 1794); Tullus Hostilius, the third king of Rome, defeating the warriors of neighboring tribes (painting by Giuseppe Cesare, 16th/17th century); assassins murder Tarquinius Priscus, the fifth king of Rome, with axes (engraving on copper by Matthäus Merian the Elder, 1630); the rape of Lucretia by Tarquinius Sextus, the youngest son of the last king of Rome, Tarquinius Superbus (painting by Tintoretto, 1559); her subsequent suicide (painting by Veronese, 1580).

753 BC	After 753 BC	7th century BC	Around 715–673 BC	659 BC	About 640 BC
Legendary date of the foundation of Rome by Romulus, who is the first king (circa 753–715 BC).	According to legend, Romulus makes the settlement a refuge for outlaws.	The legend of the rape of the Sabine women; proof that, from its early days, Rome formed alliances with other nations.	The reign of King Numa Pompilius, a Sabine, who introduces the 12-month calendar.	Under Tullus Hostilius, Alba Longa is conquered and destroyed.	During the reign of Ancus Marcius, grandson of Numa Pompilius, the port of Ostia is founded.

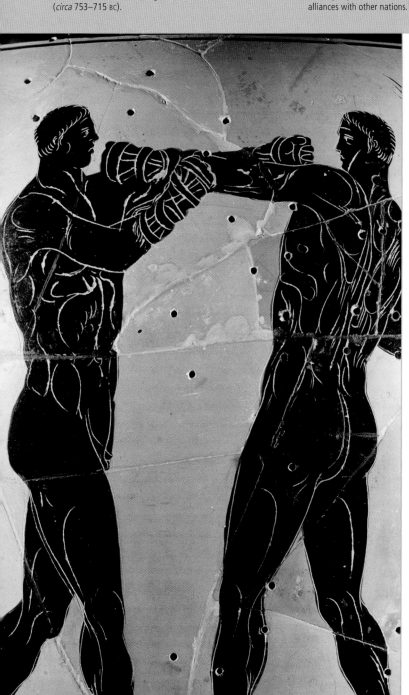

The Etruscans

The rule of the Roman kings began with Romulus. Livy narrated that Romulus declared his "city" – which is probably best imagined as a collection of small villages – to be a refuge for all those who were wandering the country, homeless for whatever reason (most had done something wrong and were on the run). The unification of separate tribes into a larger community was first brought about by the Etruscans, who came from the area north of Rome. Today, it is widely accepted that the city got its name not from its legendary founder but from the Etruscan ruling dynasty, the Ruma. It was extremely advan-

under the Etruscan kings. Among other things, they introduced drainage and water supply systems, some of which still survive, and the construction of Roman houses was strongly influenced by standard Etruscan methods. Certain traditional ceremonies can also be traced back to this time: gladiator fights are of Etruscan origin, as are circus games and the custom of building a triumphal arch for victorious commanders. The Etruscan belief system comprised a pantheon of gods and goddesses, who represented the world they

The Tomb of the Leopards (6th–2nd century BC) in the Etruscan necropolis of Tarquinia.

tageous for the development of the city that the Etruscans, who were based in the area that is now Tuscany, brought Rome under their control. Rome first blossomed

This Greek amphora, found in a town to the north-west of Rome, shows close links between Greece and the Etruscan Cerveteri.

saw around them. Tivr was god of the moon, Cathan and Usil the sun, while Turan was the goddess of love and Leinth the goddess of death. The Etruscans believed in an afterlife and consulted their deities at every turn, as did

Rome 753–509 BC
The seven kings of Rome

616 BC
Tarquinius Priscus is the first of the Etruscan rulers of Rome.

After 616 BC
Establishment of the Forum Romanum and the Circus Maximus.

565 BC
King Servius orders the construction of city walls named after him.

534 BC
King Servius is killed. His successor is Tarquinius Superbus.

509 BC
Tarquinius Superbus is overthrown as a result of his despotic rule.

After 509 BC
Rome becomes a republic, headed by two consuls (until 27 BC).

their successors, the Romans. Rome became the focal point of power for the whole region, partly because rival cities such as Alba Longa – its own "mother city" – were destroyed by the Romans. One indication that the Romans were turning their covetous eyes further afield was the creation of the sea port of Ostia in around 600 BC.

Plebeians and patricians

The growth of the population, as well as the expansion of the city's sphere of influence, demanded more than just structural developments. A "constitution" was also needed to establish the hierarchical order and define individual areas of responsibility. The king was supported by senators,

who came from the ranks of rich landowners; they called themselves patricians (sons of noble "fathers", or *patres*). This was a relatively small group compared to the large mass of plebeians – tradesmen, workers, merchants, traders, and small farmers – who had some rights, but were excluded from most forms of office.

As Etruscan-style ideas of kingship gained ground, the distance between the ruler and his subjects increased. The last of the Etruscan kings took the idea of his supremacy too far. This king, Tarquinius, was given the epithet Superbus, which means proud or arrogant. He wantonly disregarded the laws of the city, which eventually led to him being overthrown, and he, his children, and his whole dynasty were banned from Rome for ever: an early example of the truth of the saying: "Pride comes before a fall."

Giambologna's magnificent *Rape of the Sabine Women* (16th century).

Cult of the dead: this Tomb of the Priests (6th–2nd century BC) is also in Tarquinia.

Rape of the virgins

There were apparently few women among the shady characters who flooded into Rome in its early days – the large number of men gave rise to the worry that Rome would only last a generation due to a lack of descendants. To prevent this, so legend has it, a feast was arranged, to which the Romans invited many families from the Sabines, tribes from the area surrounding Rome. At the height of the feast, the Romans attacked the guests and drove them all away – except the young women, whom they held captive and kept for themselves … In the next part of the legend the Sabines attacked Rome, but the women, now married to Romans, positioned themselves among the fighting men and intervened in the battle, pointing out that they now all belonged to the same family – some as their fathers, others as their husbands – so why fight each other? It seems that the story does have a kernel of truth: the Romans and Sabines apparently coexisted peacefully in the 6th century BC, and even formed alliances at times. The Rape of the Sabine women has provided a potent inspiration for many works of art, particularly in the Renaissance. The "rape" was not the act of sexual violation by which we understand the word today, but rather a kidnapping of the women in order to ensure the continuity and survival of the new city. Many artists through the ages have portrayed the story, from Nicolas Poussin and Peter Paul Rubens to Pablo Picasso.

After the last king of Etruscan descent was overthrown, Rome became a republic. This in itself was a revolutionary notion, as until then societies had had a supreme ruler at their head as a matter of course. Even 2,000 years later the Romans of the pre-Christian period were considered pioneers of this form of government:

during the French Revolution it was said "*ainsi faisaient les Romains*" – "this is how the Romans did it". Right: Roman busts of Scipio Africanus, Hannibal, Pompey, Marcus Licinius Crassus, Gaius Julius Caesar, Marcus Junius Brutus – all great men of their times.

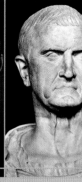

499 BC	**396 BC**	**390 BC**	**312 BC**	**264–241 BC**	**218–202 BC**
The republic of Rome is at war with the Latins.	The Etruscan city of Veii is conquered. Rome starts to become the predominant power in the region.	Rome is captured by Gauls and only released on payment of a ransom.	Construction is begun on the Via Appia and the first aqueduct to supply water to the city.	First Punic War against Carthage, Rome's competitor on the Mediterranean.	Second Punic War. The Roman general Scipio Africanus defeats the Carthaginians.

A new power

After the last king of the Etruscan dynasty was driven out, no successor was appointed; instead, Rome became a republic. From the year 509 BC, instead of a single ruler, power was in the hands of two consuls, who monitored each other and whose period in office was limited to one year. These two officials came from the patrician class –

Off to Italy: Hannibal's feared

the nobility who appointed all high officials. In later times, the plebeians – the ordinary people – frequently protested against this supremacy of a relatively small class.

Myths depicted centuries later – the consul Publius Decius Mus (died 340 BC) prophesies the victory of the Romans over the Latins (painting by Peter Paul Rubens, around 1617).

Rome 509–30 BC
The republic

"Hannibal is at the gates"

The strengthening of the state structure made expansion possible. Rome waged war on the Etruscans, who were crushed in 396 BC. Six years later, however, Brennus, a Gaulish chief, conquered Rome and released it only after receiving a large ransom. The saying *Vae victis* (woe to the vanquished) is attributed to him.

War raged (the Carthaginians were also known as Punics). It ended in the surrender of Carthage, which lost control of Sicily: the island became the first Roman province. In 218 BC, clashes flared up again. Carthage's commander Hannibal inflicted heavy losses on the Romans; but despite the legendary cry of horror "*Hannibal ante portas*" ("Hannibal is at the gates"), the Carthaginians could not capture the city. In 201 BC, Carthage admitted defeat. In

Caesar and the last years of the republic

Small farmers suffered from the many wars, as soldiers were recruited from their ranks. Their land lay fallow and they were often forced to sell to large landowners, who had sufficient slaves to be able to continue to farm profitably. This resulted in the formation of a new social class, whose members had served in the wars and now wanted to have some

increased social instability. In 60 BC, a triumvirate of three men – Pompey, Crassus, and Caesar – effectively held all political power. Crassus, notorious for having crushed the slave rebellion led by Spartacus, was one of the richest men in Rome. He was killed attempting to conquer Parthia, the empire that included modern-day Iran. The best known of the three is Gaius Julius Caesar, who became consul in that year. Caesar went on to

weapons were his legendary war elephants (fresco from the early 16th century).

"Et tu, Brute?" The murder of Gaius Julius Caesar on 15 March 44 BC by his opponents (painting by Friedrich Heinrich Füger, 1815).

Rome's great rival in the Mediterranean was the naval power of Carthage, capital city of the Phoenicians, in present-day Tunisia. In 509 BC, the Romans signed a trade agreement with the Phoenicians, but just over 200 years later any attempt at peaceful coexistence was abandoned. Between 264 and 241 BC, the First Punic

149 BC, the city was flattened by an earthquake; the surviving inhabitants were sold into slavery, and the Punic lands became Rome's African province.
One of the great generals of antiquity, Hannibal's legendary status was cemented by his amazing achievement of crossing the Pyrenees and the Alps to enter Italy with an army that included war elephants.

political influence; at the same time, impoverished small farmers streamed into Rome in vast numbers. There they soon formed a sort of urban proletariat, and this social issue threatened to upset the whole structure of the state. A bloody civil war flared up, and several slave uprisings

conquer Gaul and successfully defended the republic against the Teutons, who were pushing south. In 49 BC, he waged a civil war against Pompey, his former ally. This war ended in Caesar's victory, and from then on he ruled alone, as dictator – until he was murdered in 44 BC by supporters of the old republican system, including his friend Brutus.

After decades of internecine strife and several civil wars, costing the lives of tens of thousands of Roman citizens, it is little wonder that there awoke in even the staunchest republicans a desire for a stronger and more durable leader, a man who could guarantee political and social stability and who would *de facto* rule alone, although without abolishing certain republican structures, such as the Senate, as the final executive authority. They found this man in Caesar's great-nephew, Octavian (right; beside him are the emperors Caligula, Nero, Marcus Aurelius, Trajan, and Caracalla).

27 BC
Octavian becomes Emperor Augustus. End of the civil wars that broke out after his death.

13 BC
The Ara Pacis is erected in honour of Octavian, whose new *agnomen*, Augustus, ushered in the period of "Augustan peace".

AD 9
Three Roman legions are slaughtered in the Teutoburg Forest by the Cherusci.

About 30
Jesus of Nazareth is crucified in the province of Judea.

42
The apostle Peter arrives in Rome. Christianity finds many followers.

64
The disastrous fire in Rome under Nero's rule. First persecution of Christians, who are accused of starting the fire.

Life in ancient Rome

Trajan's Baths, and the reconstruction of the Domus Flavia (above) on the Palatine Hill, illustrate the magnificent display of urban wealth in ancient Rome.

The top strata of Roman society were the patricians who could trace their ancestry to one of the 100 patriarchs, or founders of the city. Below them came the plebeians, free-born citizens, then the freedmen (freed slaves), and finally the slaves.

Life in the capital of the Roman Empire in many respects must have been similar to life in large European cities such as London at the start of the industrial age. The *domus* – which varied in degrees of magnificence – was the palatial residence of one family and its slaves. For the lower classes there were *insulae* – tenement houses with shops and workshops on the ground floor, and modest to poor living quarters on the upper floors. Fires often broke out in these lower class districts, and a fire service, the *vigiles*, was founded to fight fire in any way they could – water generally had to be transported by hand in leather buckets. The *vigiles* had other responsibilities as well: crime was a problem in the city – there were times when well-heeled Romans would only go out at night in a litter, accompanied by armed slaves.

How Emperor Domitian's Palace might have looked in the 3rd century.

Pax Romana

After centuries of domestic political turmoil, a long period of stability dawned under Octavian, a great-nephew of Caesar, who became emperor and was given the title "Augustus" – this was the time of *Pax Romana* (also known as *Pax Augusta*, the peace of Augustus). However, foreign wars continued as before, particularly against the Germanic tribes. The province of Judea, although it had been conquered by Pompey in 63, remained a major trouble spot, which is why the prefect Pontius Pilate took draconian measures when a man called Jesus of Nazareth, preaching about love and forgiveness, found numerous followers there: it was feared that a spiritual movement could become a political one.

"Queen of Cities"

A striking number of Augustus' successors were either killed or committed suicide. Caligula (emperor between AD 37 and 41), with his delusions of grandeur and persecution mania expressed in a conviction of his own divinity, developed a megalomania, while Nero (emperor in the years 54–68) is now considered the perfect example of a megalomaniac ruler.
In 98, the Spaniard Trajan became emperor; in the hands of this experienced

67
Crucifixion of the Apostle Peter. The Apostle Paul is executed in Rome.

72
Construction begins on the Colosseum. The "games" are intended to keep the common people amused.

98
The Empire reaches its greatest geographical extent under a non-Roman ruler, the Spaniard Trajan.

161
Accession to power of the philosopher-emperor, Marcus Aurelius, author of the *Meditations*.

193–311
Over 50 "soldier emperors", chosen by the military, reign in quick succession.

324
Under Constantine the Great, Rome is divided into east and west.

The Ara Pacis Augustae, the Altar of Peace, was a symbol of the change in the nation's policies under Emperor Augustus.

Apotheosis of Sabina, the wife of the emperor Hadrian (seated), from a marble relief (136/138BC) in the Palazzo dei Conservatori.

and capable officer, the empire reached its prime. The philosopher-emperor Marcus Aurelius (161–180) wrote *Meditations*, full of wisdom and insight – in practical terms he showed himself to be less clear-minded: going against tradition, he made his inept son his successor. The military emperor Caracalla (211–217) unleashed a regime of building activity that the capital had not seen since the time of Augustus. Emperor Aurelian (270–275) again sought to strengthen the empire; emperor Diocletian (284–305) reacted strongly against revolt within the empire, justifying his position as absolute monarch. Emperor Constantine (306–337) reversed Diocletian's policies of hate and persecution, and granted Christians full religious equality under an edict of tolerance; he founded a second capital in Constantinople (today's Istanbul). The city on the Bosphorus soon began to outstrip the city on the Tiber as the "Queen of Cities".

Under Theodosius (379–395), Christianity was declared the state religion. Constantinople, also called East Rome, became the capital of the Byzantine Empire, which lasted until 1453, when it was conquered by the Turks. The West Roman Empire, on the other hand, continued to decline, and the last emperor, Romulus, was overthrown and driven out by the German commander Odoaker in 476.

Trajan's Column (2nd century) has bands of reliefs, about 200 m (650 feet) long in total, arranged in a spiral. They show the conquest of Dacia by Emperor Trajan.

"The Pope, the Bishop of Rome, and the successor of St Peter is the 'perpetual and visible principle and foundation of unity of both the bishops and of the faithful'" – at least according to the "Dogmatic Constitution on the Church of the Second Vatican Council", which is headed "Lumen Gentium"

("Christ is the light of the people"). Jesus of Nazareth, about whom Pope Benedict XVI wrote a very personal book, is considered to be the prototype of the notion of "holy office" within the church. Right: Popes Gregory VII, Innocence III, Anastasius II.

476
The last emperor, Romulus, is deposed. Rome loses importance as a world power.

496
Anastasius II is the first pope to award himself the title "Pontifex Maximus".

568
Invasion by the Germanic Lombards. Rome is officially part of the Byzantine Empire.

590–604
The papacy grows in power and influence under Gregory I; church leaders also begin to hold worldly power.

609
The Pantheon, a temple dedicated to "all gods", becomes a Christian church.

752
Stephen II asks Pepin, king of the Franks, for aid against the Lombards.

Representative of Jesus

Rome's prominent role in the Roman Catholic religion can be traced to St Peter, one of the disciples of Jesus. According to Christian tradition, he was appointed by Jesus as his successor and representative on earth and became the first bishop of

Above: The reliquary with the chains of St Peter in Vincoli's Basilica of San Pietro. Left: The statue of St Peter in front of St Peter's Basilica.

Rome. He was crucified around AD 64 on the orders of Nero, who sought to blame the Christians for the Great Fire of Rome. Early Christians had carried out their ceremonies in secret, but after the edict on tolerance was issued by Emperor Constantine, the first public Christian buildings were constructed. Work on the first St Peter's began in around 324; on Santa Maria Maggiore in 356, and on Santa Sabina in 422. Siricius (384–399) was the first Roman bishop to give himself the title "papa" (father), the origin of the word "pope".

Roman Catholics

While Rome continued to lose its importance as the focal point of political power from the early 4th century onward, it simultaneously developed into the most important place in the world for Christians, after the holy city of Jerusalem. The holders of the Holy See not only asserted themselves in their role as spiritual leaders of followers of the Christian faith, but also developed and expanded their political power.
In 754, the – Catholic – king of the Franks, Pepin III, granted the Church extensive territories on the Italian peninsula. These formed the

Rome 476–1309
The popes and the Papal States

754
The so-called "Donation of Pepin" brings the church extensive territories across the Italian peninsula.

800
Charlemagne is crowned emperor by Pope Leo III, further strengthening the Western Roman Empire.

846
Moorish troops land at Ostia and lay waste to the (first) Church of St Peter, a basilica built over what was thought to be the Apostle's tomb.

962
The German king Otto I is crowned emperor by John XII; Otto orders that the pope can only be elected with the agreement of the emperor.

1057
Stephen IX is elected pope without the consent of the emperor.

1075, 1122, 1309
The investiture controversy between worldly rulers and church leaders ends with the Concordat of Worms; the Papacy moves to Avignon.

Santa Maria in Trastevere is probably the oldest of all the churches dedicated to the Virgin and was the first site in Rome where Christians could worship in public.

Gregory I (Gregory the Great) depicted in a 15th-century fresco by Andrea Delitio in Atri cathedral.

physical foundation for the Papal States, which over the centuries extended as far as Tuscany in the north and almost to Naples in the south. In 1075, Gregory VII announced the *Dictatus Papae*, asserting that the spiritual and political powers of the pope exceeded that of any other Christian – including the emperor. The so-called investiture controversy that followed involving the secular leaders and the leaders of the Church was finally settled in 1122 with the Concordat of Worms. Theocracy reached its peak in the papacy of Innocent III (1198–1216) and Rome flourished. However, in 1309 Pope Clement V, a Frenchman, moved the papal seat to Avignon and thus into the sphere of influence of the kings of France – a temporary triumph for secular power.

In 1377, Gregory XI brought the papacy back to Rome, but the intervening decades, when Rome was not the sole seat of the leaders of Christianity, had had serious consequences for the city. The population had fallen, as had many buildings. Grass grew in the streets, and sheep and goats grazed in the heart of the city.

Right: The tomb of Sixtus VI in St Peter's. Referring to a classical Roman martyr (Sixtus II), Francesco della Rovere (born 21 July 1414 in Celle, the modern Celle Ligure in the province of Savona) took the name of Sixtus during his reign as pope (1471–1484). His incumbency is considered the beginning of a Renaissance papacy characterized by flagrant nepotism and extravagant courtly behaviour. Pope Sixtus VI was also a significant patron of the arts, sponsoring the work of the greatest painters of the time and commissioning the building of the Sistine Chapel between 1473 and 1481, among other projects.

1377	**1378–1417**	**1447**	**1473**	**1503**	**1504**
Gregory XI moves the papacy back to Rome from Avignon.	The great schism in the Church: two popes rule simultaneously, in Rome and Avignon.	Nicholas V founds the Vatican library, whose modern holdings include more than 500,000 volumes and some 60,000 manuscripts.	Sixtus VI commissions the building of the Sistine Chapel and has the walls decorated with frescoes.	Julius II lays the foundation stone for a collection of classical statuary (including the Laocoön group).	Julius II brings Michelangelo to Rome, to design his tomb.

Pope Julius II

The foundation stone for the new St Peter's was laid in 1506 by Pope Julius II (1443–1513, pope from 1502). Critics maintained that he only commissioned such a huge building in order for there to be room in it for the grandiose tomb designed for him by Michelangelo. In the event, the tomb was not quite as monumental as originally planned, and space was eventually found for it in a church of rather more modest dimensions, San Pietro in Vincoli.

Julius II went down in history not only as a patron of the arts, but also as a successful commander. He won back territories for the Papal States, and "founded a power that was never before possessed by a pope", according to the historian Leopold von Ranke.

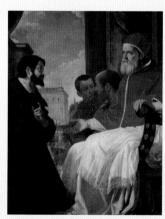

Above: Artist and patron: Michelangelo in discussion with Pope Julius II (painting, A. Fontebuoni).
Left: The recumbent figure on the tomb of Pope Julius II was created by Maso del Bosco.

The power of the popes

After his return from exile in Avignon in 1377, Gregory XI and his followers set about reviving Rome's former magnificence. The passion for ostentation of some popes knew no limits. As the Church now had enormous wealth, its leaders could employ the most important artists of their time. To decorate the Sistine Chapel – named after himself – Pope Sixtus IV brought to Rome the

Rome 1377 – 1547
The High Renaissance

1506
The foundation stone is laid for the construction of the new St Peter's, to designs by Bramante.

1508
Michelangelo starts decorating the vaulted ceiling of the Sistine Chapel.

1509
Raphael starts on the frescoes in the *stanze*, the private chambers of Julius II.

1510/11
Martin Luther visits Rome; he vehemently criticizes the situation he finds there, especially the selling of indulgences.

1527
Sack of Rome: the city is plundered by soldiers of the emperor Charles V. Pope Clement VII takes refuge in the Castel Sant'Angelo.

1547
Michelangelo is engaged as the architect for St Peter's Basilica; the dome is based on his designs.

The dome of St Peter's was designed by the great Michelangelo.

Michelangelo's frescoes in the Sistine Chapel.

The Swiss Guard

Always at the ready …

For his own protection, Pope Julius II created a bodyguard of 150 young men from the Swiss canton of Uri – the Swiss Guard. They were first deployed in the Sack of Rome on 6 May 1527 by German and Spanish mercenaries, and were almost annihilated. Today, the Swiss Guard is the last remnant of the once immense armed forces of the Papal States. The guards must be Catholic single males aged 19 to 30, with Swiss citizenship, who have an exemplary military service record.

A glimpse behind the scenes …

painters Pinturicchio, Perugino, and Signorelli from Umbria, and Botticelli, Ghirlandaio, Cosimo Roselli, and Piero di Cosimo from Florence. Later, the great Michelangelo was commissioned – by Julius II – to paint the ceiling of the chapel with the now world-famous frescoes, while Raphael decorated the pope's private chambers in the Vatican.

The reconstruction of St Peter's was the greatest project of its type for decades. Pope Julius II commissioned the architect Donato Bramante to tear down the old basilica, built in the 4th century on the site of the tomb of St Peter, and to construct a new one, a plan that encountered a great deal of resistance. In order to finance the costly new building, believers were allowed to buy "indulgences", a remission of the punishment for sin, which – in addition to the worldliness of the popes – was one of the reasons that Martin Luther demanded a reformation of the Church.

Paradoxically, further magnificent buildings were constructed during the Counter-Reformation – the papal reaction to the efforts of Luther – in order to show all believers the unbroken power of the Roman Catholic Church.

There was a cruel setback to the development of the city when Pope Clement VII became entangled in the wars between France and Spain for supremacy in northern Italy, hoping to profit by them and be able to gain new territories. In 1527, Spanish soldiers and German mercenaries conquered Rome and plundered and slaughtered the inhabitants. The pope took refuge in the Castel Sant' Angelo; but of the 55,000 or so people who lived in Rome at that time, about 33,000 were killed or abducted, or fled.

Maffeo Barberini, born on 5 April 1568 in Florence, reigned as pope from 1623 to 1644 as Urban VIII (the portrait, right, was painted by Bernini between 1625 and 1630). His incumbency as pope saw the consecration of St Peter's Basilica (1626) and the trial of Galileo Galilei (1632–1633). The pope was a great admirer of Giovanni Lorenzo

(Gianlorenzo) Bernini (1598–1680, seen center right in a self-portrait of 1635), a baroque architect of genius who now lies buried in Santa Maria Maggiore. Far right: Pope Innocence X (Giambattista Pamfili, elected pope 1644) in a 1650 portrait by Diego Velázquez.

1582
Sixtus V commissions lavish redesigns of many squares in Rome during the Counter-Reformation.

1595
Annibale Carracci decorates the interior of the Palazzo Farnese with frescoes.

1600
The monk Giordano Bruno is burnt to death on the Campo de' Fiori for heresy.

1625
Appointed by Pope Urban VIII as his court sculptor, Bernini goes on to create numerous churches, fountains, and monuments.

1626
Official opening of the new St Peter's (the foundation stone was laid in 1506).

1631
The Papal States reach their greatest extent under Urban VIII.

Giordano Bruno

Bruno – an intellectual who would later influence the spiritual life of Europe – was born in Nola, near Naples, in 1548. He entered the Dominican Order at a young age, but left, accused of heresy, and wandered through Europe. He fell into the hands of the Inquisition in Venice and was taken to

The memorial in the Campo de' Fiori to the monk and philosopher Giordano Bruno, whose pantheistic ideas were to influence important literary figures.

Rome. He was imprisoned for more than seven years, and was burnt at the stake on 17 February 1600. Giordano Bruno, who equated God with nature, did not consider himself an atheist in any way, but he held the view that God was present everywhere: "In the universe, there is no difference between the finite and the infinite, the greatest and the smallest."

A baroque view of life – the ceiling painting *The Triumph of Divine Providence* by Pietro da Cortona (1596–1669), in the Palazzo Barberini, served to glorify Pope Urban VIII and his family.

1633
Galileo Galilei, condemned to death as a heretic, retracts his "blasphemous" teaching.

1651
Bernini undertakes the refurbishment of the Piazza Navona.

1656
The plague kills around 15,000 people in Rome. The colonnades of St Peter's Square are built to designs by Bernini.

1726
The Spanish Steps are built, to designs by Francesco de Sanctis.

1732
Construction of the Trevi Fountain is begun; the work will not to be completed until 1762.

1734
Clemens XII opens the Palazzo Nuovo to all, creating the first public museum.

Heretics and believers

The flurry of building activity in Rome under Pope Sixtus V (1585–90) continued into the 17th century. The reason behind the magnificent, newly constructed churches was – according to the Holy See – to display the triumph of the true faith over heresy. If the power of

Bernini's masterpiece *The Blessed Lodovica Albertoni* (in San Francesco a Ripa).

imagery could not achieve this end, then deviation from the official line could be addressed in different ways: in 1600, Giordano Bruno, a monk who had questioned, among other things, that the earth was the hub of the universe, was burned to death in the Campo de' Fiori.
Astronomer Galileo Galilei (1564–1642), who made similar supposedly heretical assertions, escaped death because, unlike Giordano Bruno, he retracted his theses when faced with the prospect of execution.

A changing city

In 1631, under Urban VIII, the Papal States reached their greatest point of expansion. In Gianlorenzo Bernini the pope found an ingenious architect and sculptor, who understood the pope's plans to make the heart of Christianity even more impressive. Bernini created, among many other works, the Fountain of the Four Rivers in Piazza Navona and the Ecstasy of St Teresa, a statue in Santa Maria della Vittoria; he also completed the colonnaded walk around St Peter's Square. The architect Francesco Borromini, a friendly rival of Bernini, also contributed to the expansion. In the high baroque period, the Piazza Navona was given its final layout, the Spanish Steps were laid, and the Trevi Fountain was constructed. The engraver Gianbattista Piranesi recorded the changing image of the city in his *Vedute di Roma antica e moderna* (Scenes of Rome, ancient and modern).

Gianlorenzo Bernini

Born in Naples in 1598, Giovanni Lorenzo (Gianlorenzo) Bernini came to Rome in 1606 and was soon "discovered" by Pope Paul V. A brilliant architect and sculptor, Bernini made his mark on the baroque face of Rome, working for eight popes, until his death in 1680.

The design and execution of Bernini's tomb of Pope Urban VIII (in St Peter's Basilica).

Bernini's bronze baldachin for the papal altar in St Peter's is 29 m (95 feet) high.

Right: Mazzini, Cavour, Victor Emanuel II, Napoleon I, and Pius IX. Both Giuseppe Mazzini (1805–1872) and Camillo Benso, Count of Cavour (1810–1861), supported Garibaldi's struggle for Italian unification, although Cavour preferred an approach based on diplomatic skill rather than the revolutionary upheaval espoused by his colleague. Victor Emanuel II, king of Sardinia (1849–1861) and of Italy (1861–1878), allowed his minister, Cavour, a free hand in matters of unification policy. Napoleon's troops occupied the city in 1798 and Pope Pius IX, having been deposed as a political leader, retreated to the Vatican.

1798
After its capture by Napoleon's troops, a republic is proclaimed in Rome, and Pope Pius VI is forced to flee the city.

1800
The pope's successor, Pius VII, is elected in Venice.

1801
Pius VII signs a treaty with France and returns to Rome.

1807
Birth of Giuseppe Garibaldi, freedom fighter and the father of Italian independence.

1808
Rome remains occupied by the French, and the pope is once again exiled.

From 1820
Many efforts are made to unify the Italian states.

Goethe in Rome

Drawn like a magnet to Rome, Johann Wolfgang von Goethe stayed in the Eternal City from November 1786 until February 1787, and then from June 1787 until April 1788. He lived with the painter Johann Heinrich Wilhelm Tischbein on the Corso. Here he worked on *Torquato Tasso* and *Egmont* and wrote: "We go back and forth enthusiastically; I am getting to know the plans of the old and new Rome, looking at ruins and buildings, visiting one villa or another; the greatest curiosities are being dealt

Goethe in Rome, by J.H.W. Tischbein.

with slowly, I'm just keeping my eyes open, walking and looking and going back, because you can only prepare yourself for Rome in Rome". The poet was impressed with Rome, as the following sentence, noted after a walk across the Protestant cemetery, confirms: "Oh, to lie here: that would be beautiful, and infinitely more beautiful than living in Germany."

Napoleon's legacy

In 1798, Rome was captured by the French emperor Napoleon and a republic was proclaimed. After the turmoil of the Napoleonic era, calls for the unification of the country became stronger throughout Italy. The Corsican had broken down many of the long-established systems of rule and the leaders of numerous small Italian states and city states were deposed. Many Italians now yearned for a united Italy, one that could hold its own

Il Vittoriano commemorates the first king of Italy.

among the other strong European nations.

"O Roma o morte"

Some of the most stubborn opponents of unification over the next half-century were the popes, who saw that their own power – secular power in this case – was threatened. The extremely conservative position of

Il Vittoriano, the memorial to Victor Emmanuel II on the Piazza Venezia, has attractive details – but as a whole, many Romans and tourists find it too large and bombastic.

Rome 1787 – 1870
The end of the Papal States and the unification of Italy

1848
Nationalist uprising in Rome; Pius IX, who opposed the unification of Italy, has to flee.

1849
Pius IX returns to power with the help of the French.

From 1860
Garibaldi tries in vain to conquer Rome for the royalist cause.

1861
King Victor Emmanuel II is proclaimed ruler of all of Italy.

1870
The king's troops storm Rome and end the pope's rule.

From 1870
After his loss of power as a world ruler, Pius IX withdraws to the Vatican.

Pope Pius IX in matters of both faith and politics led to him being expelled from Rome. Although Giuseppe Garibaldi, the leader of the republican freedom movement, was supposed to have announced *"O Roma o morte"* – "Rome or death" – he was unable to hold the city and in 1849 Pius IX returned to the Vatican. The Nationalists finally conquered Rome in 1870, after bitter defensive fighting by the papal troops. And so the secular leadership of the popes ended after more than a thousand years.

Depicted astride his steed: Italy's national hero Garibaldi.

Though not forbidden to travel, Pius IX declared himself "a prisoner" and in order not to be seen to be accepting of the authority of the new Italian government, refused to leave the Vatican. He outlived Victor Emmanuel II by one month, dying in February 1878.

Giuseppe Garibaldi

Born on 4 July 1807 in Nice, Giuseppe Garibaldi was the son of a fisherman. He joined the Giovane Italia (Young Italy) movement in 1833 and after taking part in an unsuccessful uprising, he was condemned to death by a Piedmontese court in 1834, after which he fled to South America via France. In the revolutionary year of 1848, he made his return to Italy, and in February 1849 led the fight against the French.

The Expedition of the Thousand, famously led by Garibaldi, is legendary – a revolutionary adventure that started in the night of 5 May 1860 with the capture of two steamships in the port of Genoa. Five days later, the rebels landed on the westernmost point of Sicily. From there, they conquered the island and then moved to the mainland, where Garibaldi took his place next to King Victor Emmanuel II in Naples on 7 September. This became the turning point in the formation of a united kingdom of Italy.

However, Garibaldi's revolutionary impetuosity brought him into conflict with his former allies, and in spite of many attempts he failed to achieve his greatest goal – the march on Rome. He died on 2 June 1882 on the island of Caprera.

Garibaldi with the personifications of the cities of Venice and Rome, a 19th-century painting (Museo del Risorgimento).

Right: A Roman kaleidoscope from the worlds of film and film scores, fashion, and music. Alberto Moravia (d. 1990) is best remembered for the two volumes of his *Roman Tales*; along with Sophia Loren and Gina Lollobrigida, Claudia Cardinale is considered "the" Italian film diva, even though she was born in Tunisia. Ennio Morricone composed scores for over 500 films, including the theme from Sergio Leone's *Once Upon A Time In The West*. Silvia Venturini Fendi has found success as a fashion designer, and Cecilia Bartoli is a celebrated mezzo soprano. Eros Ramazotti is a pop and rock musician.

1871	1922	1929	1937	End of the 1930s	1943
Rome becomes the capital of a united Italy.	Fascist march on Rome; Benito Mussolini becomes prime minister.	Mussolini and a papal legate sign the Lateran Pacts; official establishment of the State of the Vatican City.	Mussolini initiates the foundation of Cinecittà, because he wants to exploit film for propaganda purposes.	Preparations begin in Rome (EUR) for a World Fair planned for 1942.	Some parts of Rome – including the working-class area of San Lorenzo – are destroyed by Allied bombers.

The talking statue

The story goes that a tailor called Pasquino, who lived in Rome in the 15th century, was well known for his sharp-tongued comments on current affairs – even the rulers of the time were often the subject of his satirical verses. In 1501, during digging work at the edge of the Piazza Navona, an ancient statue was found, which was so badly damaged that no collector was interested in acquiring it; this torso was simply left leaning up against the wall of a palazzo. The people called it the Pasquino statue, and it soon became the custom to stick notes on it at night, on which were written critical, and sometimes malicious, remarks about political decisions.

Over time, this custom was forgotten, but it was revived when Hitler visited Mussolini in Rome in 1938. When Silvio Berlusconi became Italian prime minister for the first time in 1994, it is said that a particularly large number of comments were found on Pasquino. The origins of the Italian word *pasquill* (lampoon) apparently can be traced back to this statue.

The Pasquino statue.

The Roman question

From 1861, Italy was a united country ruled by King Victor Emmanuel II, of the House of Savoy. Rome became the capital in 1871 – however, the Lombards, Tuscans, and Piedmontese expressed doubts, believing Milan, Florence, or Turin would have made a better *capitale d'Italia*. For the fascists, who came to power after World War I, there was no doubt: for them, Rome was an embodiment of the mighty ancient world empire, and the supporters of the self-styled Duce, Benito Mussolini, attempted to link themselves with this past glory.

In 1922, Mussolini organized a march, with protesters converging on the capital from all directions, in which about 26,000 of his supporters took part – he himself took the sleeper train. The ruler at the time, King Victor Emmanuel III, appointed Mussolini prime minister.

In 1929, Mussolini solved the so-called Roman question, which concerned the relationship between the Church and state, and thus the status of Rome: in the Lateran Pact, it was agreed that the pope would be the leader of an independent Vatican State. This *Stato della Città del Vaticano*, covering an area of just 44 hectares (108 acres), was all that remained of the once powerful Papal States. To celebrate the "reconcilia-

tion", Mussolini had the Via della Conciliazione built, sacrificing a large section of the medieval Borgo, between the Vatican and the Tiber. In 1937, the fascist dictator, who had learned that film was a useful medium for propaganda, founded the Cinecittà film studios; in the same year, he had numerous medieval buildings torn down, including some 20 churches, to make way for a World Exhibition

Anna Magnani in Roberto Rossellini's classic *Rome, Open City* (1945).

planned for 1942 (Esposizione Universale di Roma, shortened to EUR). On the site, he built the Palazzo della Civiltà del Lavoro, whose architecture echoed classical forms but was popularly known as the "square Colosseum". However, the Exhibition did not take place due to World War II, which Italy entered on 19 July 1940.

During the war, Rome experienced Allied bombing on a number of occasions. The San Lorenzo quarter suffered devastating damage, but on the whole the city emerged

fairly unscathed in comparison with many other European cities. After several attempts, Pius XII had Rome declared an open city – enabling enemy troops to enter without resistance, thereby protecting the city, its treasure, and its inhabitants from harm. On 4 June 1944, Rome was liberated by the advancing Allies.

The monarchy had fallen into disrepute because of King Victor Emmanuel III's indecisive position towards fascism, and in 1946 the Italians decided in a referendum to abolish the monarchy and form a republic. For administrative reasons, the country was divided into regions. Rome was not only the capital of the Italian Republic, but also the administrative heart of the region of Lazio. The city also

Rome 1871 to today
The triple capital

naturally remained the seat of the pope. So today Rome is no longer the capital of the world – *caput mundi* – but continues to be a triple capital. Although Catholicism is no longer the official Italian state religion (a concordat was signed between the state and the Vatican in 1984), the Eternal City remains the focal point of

Screen star Monica Bellucci greets her fans.

belief for more than one billion Catholics around the world. Great events such as the Giubileo in 2000 or the funeral of Pope John Paul II and the installation of his successor Benedict XVI in 2005 drew hundreds of thousands of believers and many onlookers.

Rome has hosted the annual *Festa internazionale di Roma* film festival since 2006.

The metro

A journey on the Roman underground.

Rome's underground train network has just two lines, called A and B. A third line, Linea C, running from north to southeast, from Grottarossa to Pantano, has long been planned, but the start of building work has continually been delayed. The cause is the same as the one that makes most new-build projects in the inner city very problematical: evidence of ancient culture and historical buildings that are at risk of being irretrievably lost. The digging work for the new Linea C therefore has to be carried out at the same time as scientifically supervised archeological excavations. Near to the Imperial Forums, there is now an underground museum covering some 3,000 sq m (32,291 sq feet), where the most important finds are displayed. Construction work on the long-awaited line C started in March 2007, and is scheduled for completion in the year 2011. The state-of-the-art line will be some 34.5 km (21.4 miles) long and will have 30 stations, from the east of the city to the north. The trains will be computer-controlled and driverless.

During the day, the Campo de' Fiori ("Field of Flowers") is the scene of the best-known weekly market in the city, but at night the square becomes a popular rendezvous for Roman *ragazzi* and *ragazze*.

The Fontana del Moro in front of the church of Sant'Agnese in Agone on the Piazza Navona. The foundations of the buildings around the square were once the main grandstand of Domitian's stadium.

CENTRO STORICO

Founded on the Palatine Hill, one of the seven hills of Rome, the city, now home to millions, was important even in ancient times, and was one of the founding cities of Western civilization. The hills were first settled in the Iron Age and over the centuries the "knee", the bend in the River Tiber, was settled with increasing numbers. Inevitably, as the inhabitants multiplied, so did the buildings. Today the historic area around the Piazza del Popolo, the Spanish Steps, the Piazza Venezia, and the bend in the Tiber forms the heart of the Eternal City.

In the middle of the square is an ancient Egyptian obelisk, brought to Rome by Augustus (below); at the entrance to the Via del Corso are the twin baroque churches of Santa Maria in Montesanto and Santa Maria dei Miracoli (right).

Piazza del Popolo

People approaching the city from the north in days gone by would have entered through a gate in the Aurelian Walls, the Porta del Popolo, arriving at the Piazza del Popolo. The "square of the people" we see today is the work of the architect Giuseppe Valadier, who wanted to "open up" Rome. When he started to redesign the piazza in 1816, he left the 1,500-year-old porta standing, as well as the 17th-century twin churches, Santa Maria in Montesanto and Santa Maria dei Miracoli, which flank the entrance to the Via del Corso to the south. On either side of the churches, the Via del Babuino and the Via di Ripetta lead out at an oblique angle into the very heart of the old city; the layout is known as il Tridente because the three streets diverge like the prongs of a trident, an ancient weapon used in gladiatorial combat. To the east of the square, steps lead to the Pincio Hill.

The Altar of Peace (below) is decorated with superb reliefs finely carved from Carrara marble. Allegorical scenes flank the entrance (Tellus, or Mother Earth, inset below), and the north and south walls depict a processional frieze of members of the emperor's family (right).

Ara Pacis Augustae

The Via di Ripetta leads from the Piazza del Popolo to the Tiber. Today, it is the site of two historic monuments to Augustus, Rome's first emperor: the Ara Pacis, dedicated to the emperor, and the mausoleum designed by him. The Ara Pacis, or Altar of Peace, was commissioned by the Senate in 9 BC to celebrate the triumphal return of Augustus and the end of the civil war; it was originally located on the Campus Martius. Over the centuries, the monument was scattered throughout Italy in various museums. It was reconstructed and opened to the public in its current location in 1938 and has been protected by a glass covering since 2006. The mausoleum is stylistically based on Etruscan barrow graves. Built of stone and cylindrical in shape, it housed burial chambers for the emperor and his family. It was topped with earth, planted with cypresses, and crowned with a bronze statue of the dead.

Officially, the Spanish Steps (below right) are named the Scalinata della Trinità dei Monti, after the French church at the top. At the foot of the steps, Bernini's Fontana della Barcaccia, represents a sinking boat (below left). Right: Opened in 1760, Caffè Greco has boasted some illustrious clients over the years.

Piazza di Spagna

On the Via del Babuino, the left tine of *il Tridente*, lies the Piazza di Spagna – so called because in the 17th century the Spanish ambassador had his residence here. For young Romans, this area used to be dangerous at night. Men would disappear without trace – forced into service in the Spanish army. The fountain in the square, La Fontana della Barcaccia, is said to have been commissioned by Pope Urban VIII. The popular name of the Spanish Steps, built between 1723 and 1726 by Francesco de Sanctis, is misleading: the steps connect the square with the French church of Santa Trinità dei Monti, and it was a French cardinal who suggested their construction, as a tribute to the king of France. However, the cardinal's idea was not without opposition and initially several popes refused to allow the steps to be built. The nearby Caffè Greco has been popular with booklovers for almost 250 years.

From A for Armani to Z for Zegna –
every Roman child knows the alphabet of the fashion houses. When Count
Giorgini staged a fashion show for an
international audience in Florence, it
was the start of the modern world's
love affair with Italian design and
taste. Italian fashion is one of the
country's chief exports, but inevitably
high quality comes at a price.

SHOPPING – HIGH FASHION, AND MORE

The area around Piazza di Spagna – the Via dei Condotti, the Via Borgognona, and part of the Via del Babuino – is a mecca for fashionistas. Here you will find all the great names in haute couture, such as Versace, Gucci, Prada, Armani, Valentino, and Laura Biagiotti. In 2007, Fendi opened a store on the Via Borgognona in a 15th-century villa, where her creations are displayed like works of art. The showpiece, a 9-m (29-foot) chandelier, is made from Murano glass. The luxury jeweler Bulgari has a branch at the entrance to the Via dei Condotti, also selling handbags and other accessories. If you love antiques, take a stroll down the Via del Babuino. The Via del Corso caters for fashion with a younger feel. The music shop Ricordi has a "mediastore" on this street. Also on the Via del Corso, in the Piazza Colonna, there is a branch of the upmarket department store chain Rinascente.

Not quite as exclusive, but well worth a visit, are the shops on the Via Nazionale, the Via del Tritone, and the Via Cola di Rienzo (on the other side of the river, north of Castel Sant'Angelo). For more clothes shopping try the Via del Governo Vecchio, where you can buy everything from jewelry and accessories to tailored coats and bathing suits. The prices are not the cheapest in Rome, but the charming, bustling Via del Governo Vecchio is very picturesque.

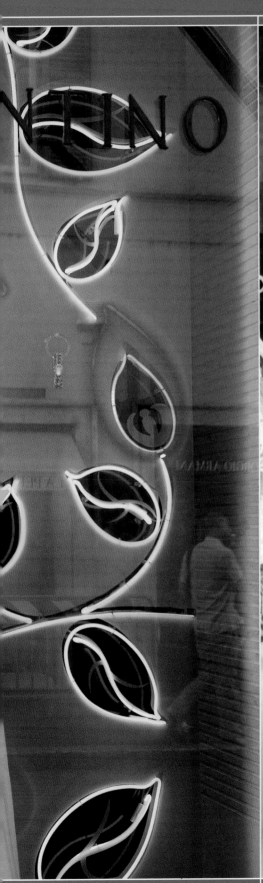

The Romans called the circular Pantheon the Rotunda. Today, the square that takes its name, the Piazza della Rotonda, constructed under Clement XI, is a hive of activity (below). The 9-m (29-foot) wide opening in the "vault of heaven" is the ancient Pantheon's sole source of light (right).

MAGRIPPA·L·F·COS·TERTIVM·FECI

Piazza della Rotonda

West of the Via del Corso, on the Piazza della Rotonda, is one of the most impressive buildings of ancient times: as its Greek name implies, the Pantheon was a temple dedicated to all the gods. This domed structure has had a varied history: built in 27 BC, it was destroyed by fire in AD 80 and reconstructed during the reign of Emperor Hadrian (117–138). The round opening in the dome, the oculus (eye), had a mystical significance, creating a link to the world of the gods. The building was closed in the 5th century but subsequently converted into a Christian church by Pope Boniface IV, who, in so doing, ensured its preservation. Used as a mausoleum from the time of the Renaissance, it houses the tombs of Raphael and Annibale Carracci, and also those of King Umberto I and Victor Emmanuel II, the first king of the united Kingdom of Italy, though it has been a republic since 1946.

The frescoes created by Raphael and his pupils in 1518 for the Villa Farnesina in the district of Travestere portray the myth of Cupid and Psyche – including the *Council of the Gods* (below). Guido Reni's fresco (1612–14) in the central hall of the Casino Rospigliosi-Pallavicini in Rome shows Apollo pursuing Aurora, the goddess of the dawn, in his chariot (right).

THE ROMAN GODS

The ancient Romans recognized many deities and also adopted foreign gods, such as the Egyptian goddess Isis. As their empire expanded, the Romans would grant equal status to the gods of the conquered lands as to their own deities, building sanctuaries for the new gods in Rome. Hence the cult of Mithras, usually depicted as a young man, arrived in Rome from Persia and was taken to parts of Germany and Britain as the Romans made their way across Europe. Up until the 5th century BC, the Roman gods were personifications of nature; then, under the influence of the Etruscans, they also accepted but renamed the Greek pantheon. Father of the Greek gods Zeus became Jupiter, and his wife Hera became Juno. The ten other chief Roman gods were: Apollo (poetry), Ceres (fertility), Diana (the hunt), Mars (war), Minerva (wisdom), Venus (love), Neptune (the sea), Vesta (the hearth and its fire), and Vulcan (fire and metal working); Mercury was the messenger of the gods, as well as the god of thieves and merchants. Other gods were added to the 12 main ones, including Bacchus, the god of wine, and Pluto, the lord of the underworld. Officially, they all stopped existing in Christian times; their temples were closed or, like the Pantheon, converted into churches. However, the old gods lived on in art and literature, and they continue to enrich our lives.

The series of three paintings produced by Caravaggio between 1597 and 1602 for the Contarelli chapel is the church's most famous work (below and right). The paintings show scenes from the life of St Matthew – *The Calling of St Matthew, The Inspiration of St Matthew*, and *The Martyrdom of St Matthew*.

San Luigi dei Francesi

This church, dedicated to French king Louis IX who was canonized in 1297, is a place of worship for French residents in Rome – the coat of arms on the gable features lilies, the emblem of France. The façade depicts French historical figures, such as Charlemagne, St Jeanne de Valois, and St Clotilde. Construction began in 1518 and after a lengthy interruption was completed in 1589, with the aid of financial contributions from the French king. The church has an opulent interior with three naves. A side chapel contains three large paintings by Caravaggio (1571–1610), depicting scenes from the life of St Matthew. Caravaggio is considered the first of the great baroque painters and a master in the use of dramatic lighting; he is well known for his *chiaroscuro* ("light-dark") painting and strong realism, as well as for the religious subjects of most of his works.

The Quirinal Palace (below: an overview and a palace guard; right: the Scala del Mascarino; far right: the Sala degli Ambasciatori) is now used as the president's official residence. It stands on the Quirinal Hill, one of the legendary seven hills of Rome, and is closed to the public.

ROME – CAPITAL OF THE REPUBLIC

Italy is a young republic: only on 2 June 1946 did a small majority of the country's citizens decide on the abolition of the monarchy. The church had spoken out in favour of the retention of the king; anything else would be a dangerous leap into the unknown. Umberto II, known as the *re di maggio* (May king) as he reigned for

only a month, went into exile. No new buildings were constructed in Rome to house the various ministries and departments of the new state, not least for conservation reasons, and centuries-old *palazzi* were chosen instead. The Quirinal Palace was selected as the residence of the "first man", the new president of the

republic. Built in the 16th century as a papal summer residence and adapted for the king's purposes in 1870, the *palazzo* is the largest Renaissance building of its kind in the world. The Minister of Foreign Affairs and his staff now reside in the Palazzo Chigi and the parliamentary chamber is located in the Palazzo Montecitorio. The

Senate sits in the Palazzo Madama. Although the politicians complain from time to time about the drafty, cramped, and antiquated conditions in these magnificent palaces that once belonged to popes and the nobility, most of them – even the socialists and communists – seem to feel quite at home there.

To finance the Fountain of the Four Rivers in 1651, special taxes were raised, including a tax on bread – not a popular move. Below left: Gianlorenzo Bernini's allegory of the Ganges on the Fountain of the Four Rivers; below right: the Fountain of Neptune. Local artists display their work in the Piazza (right).

Piazza Navona

This piazza grew into its present form over several centuries. Its elongated shape indicates that it was once a stadium, built by Caesar and expanded in the year 85 under Domitian. In the early Middle Ages, a church was built on the site where St Agnes had suffered a martyr's death; living quarters and shops were constructed under the former spectator stands, which gradually developed into larger buildings. In 1477, Sixtus IV granted permission for a market to be held here and horse races were run in the square until 1495, when it was paved. In the 17th and 18th centuries, the piazza was turned into a lake during the celebrations held by the powerful Pamphili family. In the mid-17th century, two rival architects were commissioned to improve the square: Bernini created the Fountain of the Four Rivers, and Borromini rebuilt the church of Sant'Agnese in Agone.

In the unofficial ranking of the Roman fountains, the most famous is the Fontana di Trevi (below left) – throw a coin in over your shoulder and it is said you will return to Rome one day – followed closely by the fountains on the Spanish Steps and in the Piazza della Rotonda (below right, from top). Many of the fountains boast fine sculptures and mosaics (right).

THE ROMAN FOUNTAINS

In Rome there is a fountain on almost every street corner and in almost every square – several hundred in total. The simplest consist of a bent metal outflow pipe with a small basin below. Passers-by can stop to quench their thirst at these nose-shaped pipes, which the Romans have affectionately nicknamed *nasoni* (big noses). The large, elaborate, and artistically significant fountains are a legacy of ancient times. They originated in the fountains that were built at the sites of ancient shrines once dedicated to water spirits (*nymphaea*), at the ends of the aqueducts that transported water into the city. Three of these aqueducts are still intact and continue to supply the fountains: the Aqua Virgo supplies the Trevi Fountain; the Aqua Claudia supplies the Moses Fountain; and the Aqua Augusta ends in the waterfalls by the Villa Aldobrandini in Frascati. The Trevi, Rome's best-known fountain, was built 1732–1762 by Salvi and Pannini, but others to look out for include the Fontanella delle Tiare (Fountain of the Tiaras, 1927) in the Borgo district; the Fontanella del Facchino (The Porter, 1590) in the wall of Banco di Roma on Via Lata; the Fontana di Porta Cavalleggeri (1565) in the wall near the Vatican on Largo di Porta Cavalleggeri – whose basin is an ancient sarcophagus; Fontana dei Cavalli Marini (Seahorses) (1791) at the Villa Borghese.

The lively market in the Campo de' Fiori still retains the bustling air of the medieval inns that once flourished here. In the middle of the piazza the hooded figure of Giordano Bruno watches over the square (center right); he was burned at the stake as a heretic and it is no coincidence that he is looking towards the Vatican.

Campo de' Fiori

The Campo de' Fiori is a rectangular piazza which was once used for horse racing and executions – there was a permanent gibbet on the spot. The best-known offender put to death here was philosopher Giordano Bruno, who died at the stake on 17 February 1600. He was accused of heresy as, among other things, he was a proponent of heliocentrism, publicly doubting that the earth was the focal point of the universe. A memorial to him was erected in 1884, a gift of the Freemasons in a sign of protest against the Church: Pope Leo XII had accused the members of this secret order of being "destroyers of the faith". At odds with its dark past, the piazza's name means "field of flowers", harking back to the time when the area was just a meadow. During the day, flowers and local food are sold, and at night the square becomes a popular meeting place for young Romans.

Foreigners are expressly warned against taking a car onto the streets of the eternally jammed city. Cycling is foolhardy and even by moped, despite being able to wind your way through the columns of cars and park easily, it's rarely a pleasure – there are simply too many cars and too little space and the driving style is simply too unpredictable for foreign drivers.

GETTING AROUND IN ROME

In order to protect both people and monuments from exhaust fumes, the Centro Storico has been declared a "blue zone", banned to private traffic. However, many Romans seem to know someone who works for the authorities – and over 40,000 exceptions have been granted. As an outsider, driving in Rome is a risky business. Romans, as Italians in general, like to communicate with their hands, even when driving, so foreign drivers in Rome not only need to know Italian road signs and traffic laws – a red traffic light is not necessarily a command to stop – they also need to be able to decipher the most casual hand signals. Watch out for flashing headlights, which, rather than "after you" often mean "after me", while the horn is used extravagantly by all drivers. After midnight, though there may not be noticeably less traffic, Roman traffic lights are set to flash amber, indicating that any vehicle may proceed if the way is clear. Visitors should proceed with extreme caution and are advised to explore on foot or use public transport. There are only two lines on the underground rail system, the Metropolitana, but there are numerous taxis: licensed taxis are white or yellow and have a number; avoid the unlicensed ones. If you really want to venture out onto the roads, you can rent a scooter, but even this is not recommended for non-Romans.

The dazzling white limestone monument (below and right) on the Piazza Venezia has attracted its share of flack over the years, being given derogatory names such as "the typewriter" or "the wedding cake". It took 26 years to build, and was opened in 1911. In the eastern section is the Museo Centrale de Risorgimento.

Memorial to Victor Emmanuel II

If someone shouted the slogan *"Viva Verdi!"* in the mid-19th century in Italy, they were not cheering the well-known composer but Victor Emmanuel II, who had ruled the kingdom of Piedmont-Sardinia since 1849. Many Italians wanted him to be the king *(re)* of a united Italy. The name "Verdi" was made up of the initial letters of the title that the monarch would be granted on ascending the throne: Vittorio Emanuele Re d'Italia. In 1861, the supporters of a united Italy finally had their wish and Victor Emmanuel became king of Italy. Born in 1820, he had taken part in the First Italian War of Independence with his father, Charles Albert of Sardinia, and had been the joint leader of the Risorgimento (the movement for unification) with the freedom fighter Garibaldi. The king was much loved – though this love did not necessarily extend to his memorial, designed by Giuseppe Sacconi.

Flavius Valerius Constantinus – Emperor Constantine I, the Great – commemorated the defeat of his great rival, Maxentius, with a gigantic triumphal arch erected in the year 312.

"The Colosseum tells the story of Rome's greatness and its decline more vividly than any of the written histories," the writer Mark Twain once said. "It is the worthiest symbol of both of these."

ANCIENT ROME

The 20th-century Roman writer Alberto Moravia described Rome as a city that has more monuments than houses. As early as late antiquity, people were concerned about protecting this unique legacy. In 458, the Western Roman Emperor Majorian ordered that "everything that contributes to the brilliance of the city should be maintained in good order by the zeal of the citizens". With its many splendid churches and monuments such as the Colosseum, Rome's antiquities are its greatest attraction, drawing millions every year.

A copy of the equestrian statue of the stoic philosopher and emperor Marcus Aurelius – one of the so-called "Five Good Emperors" (below, inset). The original is now in the Capitoline Museums. Michelangelo's Piazza del Campidoglio on the Capitol, once the heart of the Roman world (below and right).

The Capitol

In ancient times, there was a temple dedicated to Jupiter, the most important of the gods, on the top of the Capitol, reached along a winding path from the Forum to the south-east. Today you climb to the top from the west, up a flight of steps designed by Michelangelo, alongside which runs an older staircase leading to the church of Santa Maria in Aracoeli. Once at the top – it is the lowest of the seven hills of Rome – the visitor is in the heart of a piazza with paving laid out in a geometric pattern, also the work of Michelangelo. In the middle is the equestrian statue of Marcus Aurelius, the only equestrian bronze to have survived since antiquity – it escaped being melted down in the medieval period because it was thought that the rider was Constantine I, the first Christian Roman emperor. The Palazzo Senatorio on the piazza is the seat of the mayor of Rome.

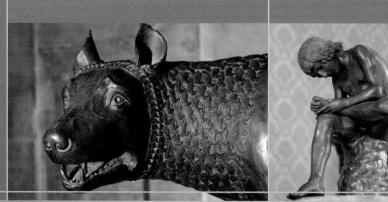

In 1734, Pope Clement XII transformed the Palazzo Nuovo, built in the previous century, into a museum. Among its ancient treasures are the remains of a colossal statue of Emperor Constantine I (below), the famous bronze *Capitoline Wolf*, and the bronze *Spinario* (right) and *The Dying Gaul* (below, inset). One of the highlights of the collection is the wonderful *Esquiline Venus* from the 1st century BC.

THE CAPITOLINE MUSEUMS

Two of the buildings in the square on top of the Capitol – the Palazzo dei Conservatori and the Palazzo Nuovo – are home to the Capitoline Museums. The collection is based on a series of ancient sculptures donated by Pope Sixtus IV and opened to the public in 1471. The best-known exhibit is the *Capitoline Wolf*, a bronze statue of the wolf who, according to legend, suckled the twins Romulus and Remus. The two human figures – sometimes ascribed to Antonio Pollaiuolo, sometimes to Gianlorenzo Bernini – are a later addition. The wolf herself was thought to be an Etruscan work from the 5th century BC, but it appears that she might not be as old as previously thought. During restoration work, it was found that the casting technique used was unknown to the Etruscans and it is now thought that it may have been produced in the Middle Ages. Another famous piece is the *Spinario*, a statue of a boy removing a thorn from his foot. The Capitoline's Pinacoteca (picture gallery) mostly contains works from the 16th and 17th centuries. Notable canvases are *The Holy Family*, by Dosso Dossi; *Head of a Boy* by Lodovico Carracci; and the fine *Double Portrait of Brothers Lucas and Cornelis de Wael*, by Van Dyck. The remains of a giant statue of Emperor Constantine (the head, a foot, hands...) are on display in the gallery's entrance courtyard.

The Roman Forum was the heart of ancient Rome (below and right). Today these ruins are evidence of the secular power of the past: the triumphal arch of Septimius Severus is flanked by the Temple of Saturn and the Temple of Vespasian, with a backdrop of the baroque Santi Lucae Martina church.

The Roman Forum

"Now I'll show you the place in the city where / Any person is most easily found, / So that you do not have to spend much time running about when you / Want to meet him, whether he's a rogue, or whether he's an honest man," wrote the poet Plautus (250–184 BC). He was speaking of the Roman Forum (Forum Romanum) – the complex of squares and buildings (erected from the 6th century BC onward) situated between the Palatine Hill and the Capitol. The Forum was full of people every day – it was here that religious ceremonies and political meetings took place, speeches were made, and goods were sold. The building complex included the Regia, a royal residence, and the House of the Vestal Virgins. When the Roman Empire fell, the Forum buildings fell into decay. In the Middle Ages, the square was known as Campo Vaccino, the cow pasture.

Located between Trajan's Forum and the lower slopes of the Quirinal Hill, Trajan's markets were the precursor of the shopping mall (below). Built in the early 2nd century, the market had some 150 shops on the lower level and offices on the upper level. Right: Relief on Trajan's Column, made from 17 blocks of marble.

The Imperial Forums

By the end of the republican era, despite various civil wars that had taken place over 60 or so years, the population of Rome had grown so much that the Forum, then about 500 years old, was no longer large enough. Caesar carried out an initial expansion in 54 BC, financing the work with booty recovered from the war against the Gauls. Around 50 years later, with the population approaching one million, Emperor Augustus further expanded the area. In AD 97, under Emperor Nerva, the square in front of a temple to Minerva was added. A final phase of expansion took place under Emperor Trajan, who ruled between 98 and 117. A 38-m (124-foot) high column was erected in the forum named after him; it is decorated with a long spiral relief celebrating his two victorious military campaigns against the Dacians, though most of the carving depicts the Roman army in action.

Fresco in the Domus Augustana, the lavish palace built by Emperor Domitian, *circa* 30 BC (below left), and painted terracotta reliefs from the Temple of Apollo, *circa* 36 BC (below right), on the Palatine Hill. Right: The Farnese pavilions were built in the 16th century for a large private garden on the Palatine.

The Palatine Hill

The Palatine Hill, the legendary site of the foundation of the city, bears the oldest traces of human settlement in Rome, dating back to the 10th century BC. Of the seven classic hills of the city, it became the place of choice for the rich and famous of ancient times on which to build their lavish residences. The statesman and great orator Cicero settled here, as did the poet Catullus. The Palatine Hill was also the home of Emperor Augustus and his wife Livia. Later emperors, such as Tiberius, Caligula, and Domitian also enjoyed living out their supremely luxurious lifestyles in magnificent palaces on the hill, but many have not survived. Domitian built the Domus Flavia for state purposes and the Domus Augustana as a private palace. The remains of the former residence of the emperor Tiberius are now covered by the Farnese Gardens, which were laid out in the 16th century.

The *velarium* was a giant retractable canvas awning that could be extended to cover two-thirds of the arena, to protect spectators from the sun or, less frequently, the rain. The emperor, city administrators, and vestal virgins sat on a podium reserved for them, while the senators had to make do with rows of ivory armchairs.

The Colosseum

Emperor Nero's palace once stood on the site of this vast ancient arena. It was one of the many wooden buildings destroyed in the Great Fire of Rome in 64 BC, which famously occurred during Nero's reign. In around AD 72, his successor Vespasian commissioned the three-floor stone arena, the remains of which can be seen today. Construction was partially financed by the treasure that the Romans plundered from the temple at Jerusalem.

When finished, the building was capable of seating 50,000 to 70,000 spectators. The games held to mark the official opening of the Colosseum lasted 100 days, during which thousands of animals were killed for the amusement of the baying crowds. The poet Martial (40–102) paid tribute to the emperor Vespasian with the following lines: "Rome has returned to its people, and under your government, Emperor, people are being entertained."

Although Constantine attributed his victory over Emperor Maxentius to a vision of Christ, his triumphal arch (below) does not display any Christian iconography. Instead, reliefs and statues were plundered from older memorials from the times of Trajan, Hadrian, and Marcus Aurelius (right).

The Arch of Constantine

The custom of erecting a triumphal arch for victorious commanders was introduced to Rome by the Etruscan kings. One of the greatest of these memorials stands near the Colosseum: the Arch of Constantine was erected to honour Constantine I by the Senate in AD 315, three years after the emperor's victory over his rivals. It was Constantine who was the first to give full recognition to Christianity as a religion. Some of the structural elements were taken from memorials dedicated to former Roman rulers: the statues of four prisoners on the north side of the arch, for example, came from a memorial to Emperor Trajan; the reliefs below were taken from a memorial to Marcus Aurelius. Reliefs inside the arch tell of Trajan's victory over the Dacians. The arch spans the Via Triumphalis, the route taken by victorious military commanders awarded a triumph by the city.

It is not certain after whom or what the Largo di Torre Argentina square was named (below and right) – perhaps after Johannes Burkard, a papal master of ceremonies (*argentoratum* in Latin) who once lived nearby, or after the silversmiths' shops in the area (*argentarii*).

Largo Argentina

Four temples from the republican, pre-empire era are to be found in this former *area sacra* (holy area) as well as the remains of the "Teatro di Pompey". The oldest temple, dedicated to Feronia – revered as the protecting goddess of all freed slaves and the guardian of the springs in the city – is thought to have been constructed in around 300 BC. Another temple was probably built to celebrate the victory of Catulus over the Carthaginians in 241 BC.

The square is part of the Campus Martius (The Field of Mars), an area of publicly owned land used as a place of public assembly and for military parades. Today the locals call Largo "the Cats' Forum", because large numbers of cats live around the ancient ruins. In 2001 the cat population in the old city was officially recognized as a "biocultural legacy" – *i gatti* enjoy special protection and are cared for here in the Largo Argentina by volunteers.

Next to the Teatro di Marcello are three Corinthian columns and a section of a frieze (below). They originally belonged to the Temple of Apollo, in which the Romans stored many of the works of art they stole from the Greeks in the 2nd century BC, prompting the vogue for all things Greek in Rome.

Teatro di Marcello

Several temples had to be demolished to make way for this theater on the ancient Campus Martius (Field of Mars). Planned by Julius Caesar, it was completed by Emperor Augustus, who named the building after his nephew, his designated successor, who had died young. The building could hold 15,000 spectators and for some events it could take as many as 20,000. Nevertheless, it was one of the smallest of its kind in Rome. It was used as a theater until around AD 400; after that time, its walls were plundered for stone for other buildings until the Savellis, one of the noblest families in the city, ordered its conversion into a fortress in the 13th century. Later, the two floors of arcades were shored up from the outside and apartments built on top; in the 16th century it became a giant palace for the Orsinis, another noble family.

According to legend, if a liar places a hand in the Bocca della Verità (Mouth of Truth), it will bite off their fingers (below). Right: The 6th-century church of Santa Maria in Cosmedin. In the 16th century, the last Roman Catholic archbishop of Canterbury, Cardinal Reginald Pole, was made a titular deacon of the church.

Forum Boarium, Santa Maria in Cosmedin

From the city's earliest days, there were many places in which the people could gather together in addition to the Forum Romanum, most of which were devoted to the sale of food, household goods, or domestic animals. The most important were the Forum Holitorium, the vegetable market, and the Forum Boarium, the cattle market. Both were located close to the ancient port on the Tiber, where there was also a temple (later converted into a Christian church) devoted to Portunus, the patron saint of ports. The area that once made up the cattle market is today called the Piazza della Bocca della Verità – named after a stone mask of a Triton (god of the sea) dating from the 4th century BC, built into the portico of the church of Santa Maria in Cosmedin. The ancient stone is said to have once been a cover for a drainage channel – a somewhat mundane use for the effigy of such a mighty god.

Professional fighters, the gladiators fought each other or wild animals, sometimes to the death, for the entertainment of the crowds. Though technically slaves – they were normally prisoners of war, criminals, or slaves – successful gladiators could buy their freedom after three years. Some men volunteered to fight as gladiators, drawn by the prospect of fame or money, as they were allowed to keep the money they won.

THE ROMAN ARENA

One of the first great pleasure palaces constructed for the people was the hippodrome, the Circus Maximus, dating from the 4th century BC. Light, two-wheeled chariots raced around the oval arena, pulled by two to seven horses. Fatal crashes were quite common, though on the whole it was a less gruesome entertainment than the so-called games held in the large amphitheaters. Built between AD 72 and 80, the largest of these, the Colosseum, was particularly famous. It could seat around 50,000 spectators – or as many as 70,000 according to some estimates. The seating was strictly regimented: the best seats, identified by name, were reserved for the senators, while women were seated at the top in the worst seats. At the official opening of the Colosseum, some 3,000 gladiators lost their lives, and countless animals were slaughtered – many imported from Africa for the purpose. Gladiators fought against each other in the arena, and if the emperor gave the infamous "thumbs down" sign, the loser was killed by the victor. The origin of gladiatorial combat is thought to lie in battles fought by slaves forced to fight to the death at the funerals of distinguished aristocrats in the 3rd century BC. The combats gradually became divorced from the funeral ceremonies and were seen as a way for wealthy citizens to proclaim their power.

A marble bust of Emperor Caracalla (below left), who sought to win over the people by building the Caracalla Baths; mosaic floors and frescoes created a sophisticated atmosphere for bathers (below center and right). A park was created on the site in around 1900 (right).

Terme di Caracalla

The Romans had a well-developed bathing culture. As early as the 2nd century BC, public bathing facilities were widely available. The emperors knew that they could buy the goodwill of the people by constructing public facilities such as baths. Entry was free, and they were used both for personal hygiene and as places for sport and leisure. One of the great bathing complexes was the Caracalla Baths (Terme di Caracalla), which could cater for 1,600 at a time, and up to 6,000 people visited the facilities daily. Inside the Terme di Caracalla were a *caldarium* (a room with hot, moist air), a *tepidarium* (a warm room), *frigidarium* (a cold room), covered walkways, a gymnasium for wrestling and boxing, a swimming pool, and other facilities. Heating was provided by a hypocaust, a system by which heat created by burning wood and coal was spread under a floor raised on pillars.

Rome can thank the Aurelian Walls for its survival over the centuries (below). They defined the boundary of the city and performed a significant defensive role until the 19th century. The Porta San Sebastiano leads out onto the Via Appia Antica (below, inset). The Pyramid of Cestius (right) stands on the road to Ostia.

The Aurelian Walls

After Rome was invaded by the Gauls in 370 BC, the Servian Walls were erected, the first defensive walls to be built around Rome. They were 11.5 km (7 miles) long and had 16 gates and were made from huge stone blocks. Construction of a new wall began in the time of Emperor Aurelian (270–275) and was completed under his successor Probus. From the dimensions of the Aurelian Walls, it is evident just how much larger and more powerful Rome had become since the city was attacked by the Gauls: the new walls were 18 km (11 miles) long, 17 m (55 feet) high and 4 m (13 feet) wide, and had no less than 381 towers. Parts of the walls are still standing today. An unusual structure was incorporated into the walls: the Pyramid of Cestius near the Porta San Paolo is the tomb of Caius Cestius Epulonius (died 12 BC) and is a reminder of the enthusiasm for Egypt at that time.

One of the most important roads in ancient Rome, the Appian Way, with its original paving stones lined with cypresses and pines, evokes images of ancient times when Romans buried their dead here at night (below and right). In 73 BC, 6,000 of Spartacus' defeated slave army were crucified along this road.

Via Appia Antica

The Via Appia, constructed in 312 BC, served as both a military and a trading route. Extended many times over the centuries, it led across the Italian peninsula to Brindisi. In around 450 BC, it was forbidden to bury the dead in the city, so the inhabitants of Rome began to inter their loved ones beside the arterial roads, which is why the Via Appia is lined with numerous family and communal graves. Today, the official start of the Via Appia is no longer in the Roman Forum, but at the Porta San Sebastiano, the city gate in the Aurelian Walls. Approximately 3 km (2 miles) out from the city is an imposing circular stone building, some 20 m (65 feet) in diameter. It contains the tomb of Cecilia Metella, the wife of a patrician. Beneath the ground on either side of the Via Appia, a network of labyrinthine catacombs, the burial place of the early Christians, is spread out beneath the fields.

The tomb of Pope Pius XI in St Peter's Basilica (below, inset): Pius signed the Lateran Pacts between the Holy See and the Italian state on 11 February 1929, guaranteeing the Holy See's international sovereignty (with the Vatican City as a new state and the pope as its leader). Below: A view across the Tiber to St Peter's.

THE VATICAN

The Via della Conciliazione, begun by Mussolini in 1937, connects St Peter's Square to the Castel Sant'Angelo on the western bank of the Tiber. The road is not only a physical link between Rome and the Vatican City, but also a symbol of the reconciliation (*conciliazione*) between the Church and state achieved through the Lateran Pact of 1929. The popes having lost their power as secular rulers in 1870, the Pact recognized the Vatican as an independent state, and the pope still bears the title "Sovereign of the State of the Vatican City".

Benedict XVI during the Easter mass, giving the *Urbi et Orbi* blessing (below). Right: St Peter with Leo III and Charlemagne; the penitent King Henry IV at Canossa; Boniface VIII at a convocation; Martin V and King Sigismund at the Council of Constance; Pius IX; John XXIII; John Paul II.

THE PAPACY – IN THE FOOTSTEPS OF ST PETER

The papacy has enjoyed a longer tradition than any other institution in the world. Uniting over one million Catholics in their faith, it is global in the best sense of the word. Its ceremonies and rituals are carried out with pomp and magnificence, setting them apart from everyday life. Today, the papacy enjoys a good reputation, but this has not always

been the case. In his role as head of the Roman Catholic Church the pope is the focal point of the Catholic religion, therefore the reputation of the papacy and the Catholic Church is inextricably linked with the character of the man holding the office. Unfortunately not all popes in the past were of good character. Renaissance popes, such

as Alexander VI (1492–1503), were notorious in their extravagance and lust for power, and some did not follow their own teaching, their real interest lying in the power of the high office, rather than proclaiming the word of God. Yet among the fallible, there were also many good men, popes who were able to effect renewal and

reform, and so papal history is marked by highs and lows. As the first bishop of Rome, Peter was also the first to hold the title of pope. According to the words of Jesus taken from the Gospel and inscribed on the internal frieze of the great dome of St Peter's: "You are Peter, the Rock, and on this rock I will build my church" (Matthew 16,18).

Monumental architecture: a view of St Peter's through the colonnades (below). In the middle of the square is a 25-m (82-foot) Egyptian obelisk, brought to Rome from Heliopolis by Emperor Caligula in AD 37. The dome of St Peter's Basilica (right), designed by Michelangelo, is a prominent feature of Rome's skyline.

St Peter's Square

The square is at its most beautiful when the sun has set, the crowds of tourists have gone, and the Roman night sky bathes the city in a magical light. It was created at the height of the baroque period, after Luther's Protestant Reformation, when the Catholic Church wanted its sacred buildings to inspire awe in believers and reinforce its claim as the one true authority of God on earth. St Peter's Square was accordingly transformed into a stunning fore-court to St Peter's Basilica. Designed by Bernini between 1656 and 1667, the square is 240 m (263 yards) wide, surrounded by colonnades of 284 columns topped by 140 statues of saints. To the left and right, at the two focal points of the giant oval, are two 14-m (46-foot) fountains. White marble sundial markers indicate the point where the tip of the obelisk's shadow lies at noon, as the sun enters each of the signs of the zodiac.

Master of central-plan building

No other architect interpreted the notion of the rebirth, or Renaissance, of classical antiquity as radically as Donato Bramante (*circa* 1444–1514). He was a master of central-plan building, in which everything referred to a central, vertical axis, as opposed to the longitudinal construction of basilicas, for example. Central-plan building achieved its apotheosis in round buildings: the Pantheon in Rome was the classical model for Bramante's Tempietto, also in Rome, an exceptional example of Renaissance architecture. The structural ideals of central-plan building outlasted the Renaissance into the baroque period. His work in Milan and Pavia had already brought him fame as an architect by the time he came to

Donato Bramante (fragment of a fresco in the Casa Grattaroli in Bergamo).

Rome in 1499, and in 1503 he entered the service of the new pope. Under Julius II, Rome once again became the artistic capital city it had been in classical times; the construction of St Peter's was undertaken in earnest and Bramante was charged with its completion. Nonetheless, his designs for a monumentally large central building in the shape of a giant square were not executed as he had planned. For liturgical reasons, and to fit more people into the church, the traditional form of a longitudinal building was adopted after Bramante's death, and thus the small, "classical" temple in the courtyard of the monastery of San Pietro in Montorio in Rome was to remain the architect's masterpiece.

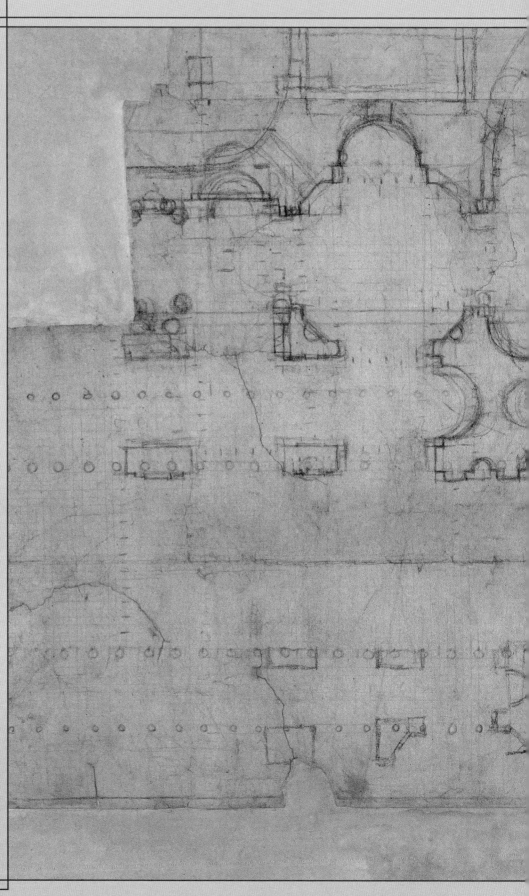

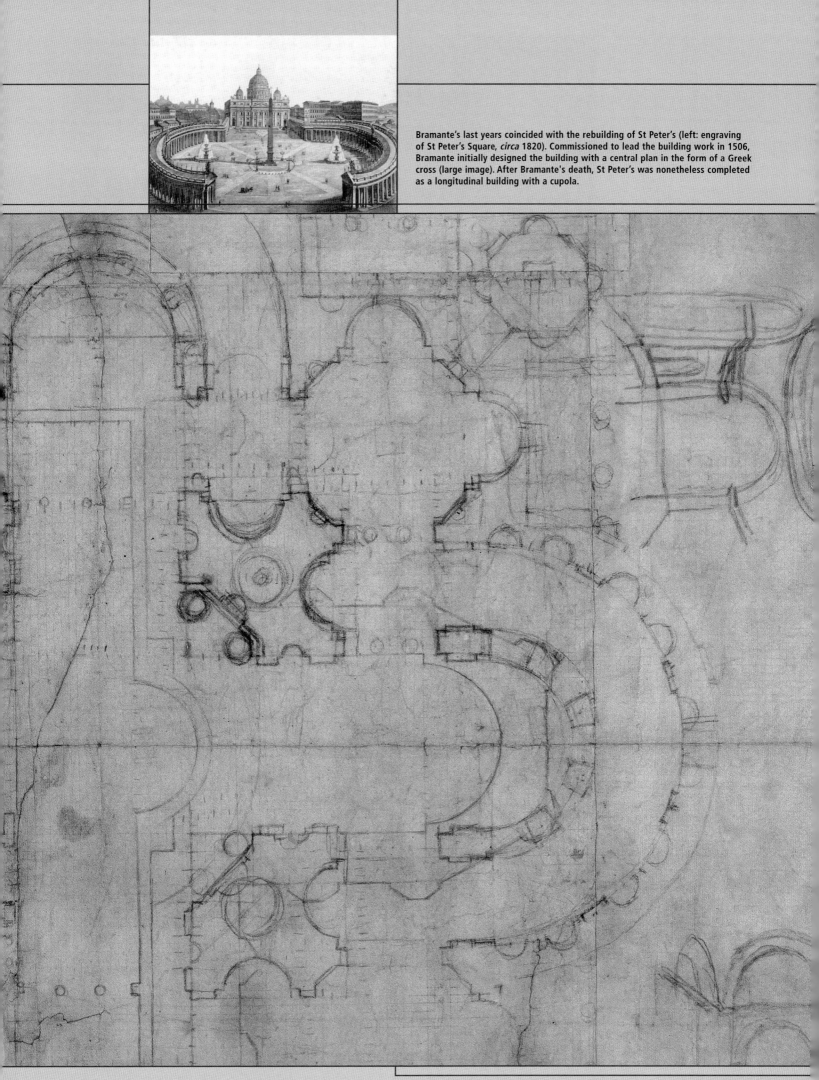

Bramante's last years coincided with the rebuilding of St Peter's (left: engraving of St Peter's Square, *circa* 1820). Commissioned to lead the building work in 1506, Bramante initially designed the building with a central plan in the form of a Greek cross (large image). After Bramante's death, St Peter's was nonetheless completed as a longitudinal building with a cupola.

By the end of the 15th century St Peter's was in a state of disrepair. Reconstruction began in 1506 and took around 150 years. Despite the number of architects involved, it retains a harmonious air (below). Right: window depicting the Holy Spirit as a dove; Bernini's altar baldachin; St Peter with the key.

St Peter's Basilica

The present basilica, which has stood since the 16th century on the site of a former basilica built under Emperor Constantine, was for many years the largest Christian church in the world. The façade is some 45 m (147 feet) high and 115 m (377 feet) wide. The lantern crowning the dome, at some 132 m (433 feet), bathes the interior in a gentle, mystical light. The interior of the cathedral can hold 60,000 worshippers. The most famous artists of their time worked on the design, including architects Bramante and Sangallo, painters Michelangelo and Raphael, and sculptors Bernini and Maderno. Near Bernini's tomb of Urban VIII you can descend to the grottoes, where the tomb of St Peter himself is said to lie. In all there are some 100 tombs located within St Peter's, including over 90 popes, and James Francis Edward Stuart, the "Old Pretender", Catholic son of the deposed James II of England.

The genius of the Renaissance

Along with Leonardo da Vinci, Michelangelo Buonarroti (1475–1564) is the most important artist of the Italian high Renaissance. Michelangelo learned fresco painting as a pupil of Domenico Ghirlandaio and looked to the old masters for inspiration, studying the sculptures of the ancient world. The creative focus for this brilliant painter, sculptor, and architect was the human figure. In order to achieve perfection in his representation of human anatomy, he is said not only to have drawn from life, but also to have secretly dissected corpses. In 1505 Pope Julius II summoned the artist to Rome to design a prestigious papal tomb, but when both this commission and his plans for a new St Peter's

Michelangelo, a portrait of the artist by one of his pupils, painted around 1510.

Basilica were rejected, Michelangelo returned, disenchanted, to Florence. However, a new challenge was to draw him back to Rome: the repainting of the ceiling of the Sistine Chapel. Michelangelo spent four years on this project, working virtually alone. High above ground balancing on a scaffolding, the work was also physically demanding. In 1547, he took over the supervision of the rebuilding of St Peter's Basilica, its dome being undoubtedly his greatest architectural achievement. Michelangelo's masterpieces as a sculptor include the *Pietà* in St Peter's and the figure of *David* in front of the Palazzo Vecchio in Florence (today, the original is in the Galleria dell'Accademia).

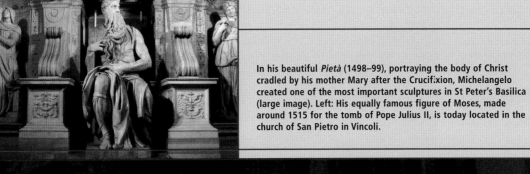

In his beautiful *Pietà* (1498–99), portraying the body of Christ cradled by his mother Mary after the Crucifixion, Michelangelo created one of the most important sculptures in St Peter's Basilica (large image). Left: His equally famous figure of Moses, made around 1515 for the tomb of Pope Julius II, is today located in the church of San Pietro in Vincoli.

The side walls of the interior of the Sistine Chapel show scenes from the lives of Christ and Moses. On the end wall is Michelangelo's altar fresco, *Last Judgement* (below, inset); his ceiling fresco (right: *The Creation of Adam*) depicts the creation and the fall of man.

The Sistine Chapel

The Sistine Chapel is where the cardinals hold papal conclaves, the ceremony in which a new pope is elected. Commissioned by Pope Sixtus IV in 1477, after whom it is named, it was originally built as a fortress as much as a place of devotion, with walls 3 m (nearly 10 feet) thick. Sixtus had been at war with the republic of Florence, but by the time the chapel was completed, in 1480, the war was over and as a gesture of peace Lorenzo de' Medici, the ruler of Florence, sent some of his city's leading painters to Rome to decorate the chapel. The artists included Perugino, Botticelli, and Ghirlandaio. The walls were painted with scenes from the lives of Jesus and Moses, and the barrel-vaulted ceiling was transformed into a radiant blue sky with golden stars. Some 20 years later, Pope Julius II commissioned Michelangelo to repaint the ceiling, the work taking from 1508 to 1512.

Below, from left: The marble Laocoön group (1 BC); a bust of Caesar; the crucifixion of St Peter (Guido Reni, 1604/1605). Right: Sufficient time should be allowed to see the Vatican museums; the recommended tour is seven kilometers (four and a half miles) long.

The Vatican Museums

Many popes were avid collectors, while others commissioned works of art in the role of both patrons and clients. Today, the complex of Vatican Museums holds one of the largest art collections in the world, ranging from ancient Egyptian and Etruscan objects to modern sacred art. The Pinacoteca (art gallery), opened by Pius XI in 1932, displays paintings from the 12th to the 19th centuries. The Missionary-Ethnological Museum brings together objects from around the world, from wherever the Catholic Church has been active. The Historical Museum has a collection of cars and carriages used by popes and cardinals, along with other objects and documents. In 2000, John Paul II officially opened the new entrance to the complex, featuring a huge spiral ramp reminiscent of New York's Guggenheim Museum. In his inaugural speech, John Paul II called the Vatican Museums "a bridge to the world".

In search of beauty

Three geniuses left their mark on the Italian high Renaissance: Leonardo da Vinci, Michelangelo, and Raphael. Born in Urbino in 1483, Raphael's fame outshone that of any other painter for centuries, and no other artist was so widely imitated. The two charming putti that Raphael added to his *Sistine Madonna* have been reproduced on millions of greetings cards and souvenirs (the original is located in the Gemaldegalerie, Dresden, Germany). Raphael's work was famous for its perfection and grace – the men and women in Raphael's paintings seem almost too beautiful to be true. He was accused by some of superficiality and sugary sweetness, but Raphael worked with the intensity and individuality of a true

Raphael's self-portrait (*circa* 1506).

master, especially in regard to his portraits. He spent several years working in Florence, then moved to Rome in 1508, when, at the height of his creativity and inundated with commissions, Pope Julius II commissioned him to paint frescoes in a suite of rooms now known as the stanze. In 1514, he took over the management of the rebuilding of St Peter's Basilica, and in 1515 he was also given the responsibility of excavating and recording Roman antiquities. When he died of a fever in 1520, he was just 37, yet he had achieved fame and recognition throughout Europe.

Among other works, Raphael created the *Fire at the Borgo* (1514, below) and *The School of Athens* (1510–1511, left) for the Vatican. The large image shows Leo IV (pope 847–855) giving his blessing from the benediction *loggia*, extinguishing the fire and miraculously saving the church and the people. *The School of Athens* assembles the greatest philosophers of antiquity in an enormous building which recalls Bramante's designs for St Peter's. The central figure of Plato is recognizable by his *Timaeus* dialogue, which discusses the nature of the universe. Raphael also immortalized himself and his master, Perugino, in the picture.

LEO · PP · IIII ·

In 1667, Pope Clement IX commissioned Bernini, master of the baroque, to create the white marble angels for the Ponte Sant'Angelo, the bridge that leads to the Castel Sant'Angelo (below and right). Each of the angels carries an instrument of the Passion of Christ (below, inset).

Castel Sant'Angelo

Emperor Hadrian (76–138) built the Castel Sant'Angelo as a mausoleum, but over the years it became a papal fortress. In the 13th century, a secret passage, the Passetto di Borgo, was constructed to connect the fortress with the papal palace. It was put to good use during the Sack of Rome in 1527, when Pope Clement VII and his cardinals escaped from the soldiers of Holy Roman Emperor Charles V. Almost all the Swiss Guard was massacred as they fought to buy time for the fleeing pope. The Castel itself survived the attack – among its defenders was sculptor Benvenuto Cellini, who killed so many enemy troops that he later suffered pangs of remorse. However, as Cellini wrote, the pope "raised his hand and made the sign of the cross over my whole body, blessed me and forgave me all my murderous deeds that I had ever committed in the service of the Apostolic Church".

The fine Venetian mosaics in the apse show Christ with Peter, Andrew, Luke, and Paul; the tomb of St Paul is said to lie under the altar (below left). Below right: the stunning coffered ceiling; right: the mosaics on the façade. The central nave's 80 granite columns date from the 18th century.

San Paolo fuori le Mura

As well as St Peter's, Rome has three other patriarchal basilicas, defined as churches that have a papal throne and an altar at which only the pope may read the mass: San Paolo fuori le Mura, Santa Maria Maggiore, and San Giovanni in Laterano. As its name indicates ("basilica outside the walls"), San Paolo fuori le Mura lies to the south, beyond the city walls. It is dedicated to St Paul, who died a martyr's death in Rome, and who is said to be buried here. The vast basilica, founded in the 4th century, was almost completely destroyed by fire in July 1823, but has been faithfully reconstructed using materials from many countries, including Egyptian alabaster pillars and Russian lapis lazuli and malachite. The 20th-century main door incorporates part of the original door, which is 1,000 years old. The 13th-century cloisters, with brightly decorated, elaborately shaped columns, survived the fire.

The basilica today is a tapestry of different artistic and architectural styles. The interior, with its three naves, reflects its original form (below). The bell tower was added in the Middle Ages, and the coffered ceiling (right) dates from the Renaissance. The domes and façade are baroque in style.

Santa Maria Maggiore

Legend has it that in 352 the Virgin Mary appeared to Pope Liberius in a dream, and commanded him to build a church in the place where he saw snow fall the next morning. Snow is a strange sight in Rome at any time of year, and it is quite miraculous when it occurs – as in this case – on 5 August. When he awoke and saw the peak of the Esquiline Hill covered in a layer of white, Liberius lost no time in obeying the will of the Virgin. To commemorate the miracle, a service takes place every August in which white petals are scattered down on the worshippers. One of the four papal basilicas, it was used as a temporary papal residence when the Lateran Palace, the principal residence of the popes before they moved to the Vatican, fell into disrepair during the Avignon papacy. Despite being damaged in the earthquake of 1348, it retains the core of its original structure from the 5th century AD.

The basilica has seen many important events: in 1929, the Lateran Treaty was signed here, and on 2 April 2007 a mass took place during the case for the beatification of Pope John Paul II. Below right: The octagonal baptistery. Right: The Holy Staircase, reputedly from Pontius Pilate's palace.

San Giovanni in Laterano

The district in which this basilica lies is named after the once powerful Laterani family, who worked as administrators for the emperors. The family was disgraced at the start of the 4th century when one of them was accused of conspiring against Nero. Their land confiscated, it fell into the hands of Emperor Constantine, who built the first Christian basilica in Rome on it. For Catholics, the Lateran basilica is the "mother of all churches", ranking even higher than St Peter's. It burned down twice, but was reconstructed on each occasion. Baroque architect Borromini altered parts of the interior in 1646 and in the 18th century the huge façade was added. The church lies on the southern side of the Palazzo Lateranense, the papal residence until the start of the 14th century. The Scala Santa (Holy Staircase), opposite the palace, is a place of pilgrimage – pilgrims must climb it on their knees.

When night falls, "the *trattoria* is filled with animalistic and salutary noise, the sounds of women laughing, glasses clinking, and children screaming, for a Roman family eats out with its restless offspring, including the babes in arms, who are breast-fed even as the mother empties a plate of spaghetti". (Colette, 1915)

FROM TESTACCIO
TO TRASTEVERE

Rome is a city of contrasts. Not only do old and new collide, but as you move from one part of the city to another you enter different worlds. A working-class district such as Testaccio is full of life and energy, while the Aventine Hill is so quiet you could almost forget you are in a city at all. On the outskirts of the city are the Renaissance and baroque villas of noble families and senior clergy, with their ornate architecture and lavish gardens. Further out, you can see the 20th-century official urban housing developments known as *borgate*.

The area around the Via del Portico d'Ottavia is characterized by restaurants and picturesque courtyards (below). Right: The Fontana delle Tartarughe (Fountain of the Tortoises) in the Piazza Mattei; sculpture in a rear courtyard; stone plaques on the Via della Reginalla; busts on the Casa di Lorenzo Manilio.

The former ghetto

For many years, Roman Jews suffered little repression, but in 1555 they were forced by Pope Paul V to resettle in a particularly unhealthy area on the banks of the Tiber. The ghetto's population numbered around 4,000, all crammed onto a small piece of land surrounded by a high wall. Life was difficult, and when the Tiber flooded the people were forced to vacate the lower floors of their tenements. A curfew was in operation, obliging the Jews to remain in the ghetto at night, and certain professions were forbidden. On Sundays they were forced to listen to a Christian priest – a practice that continued until 1848. The ghetto itself remained until the pope lost his secular authority over Rome in 1870. As a symbolic gesture, the ghetto wall was torn down. The Portico d'Ottavia, in the heart of the former ghetto, dates from the 2nd century BC. Emperor Augustus had it dedicated to his sister Octavia.

For Rome, originally founded where the Tiber flows around in a bend at the so-called "knee", the Tiber was crucial for trade and commerce.
Right: The Tiber as a symbolic fountain figure in the Piazza del Campidoglio; brave (or foolhardy) young Romans traditionally celebrate the New Year by jumping in the river.

The Tiber

The Tiber, cloudy and grey, flows erratically and "often causes great damage". This was the harsh verdict of Swiss scholar Johann Jacob Grasser in a travel guide of 1609. The third-longest river in Italy, the Tiber rises in the Apennines and drains into the Tyrrhenian Sea. In order to control its flow, or overflow, as it flooded regularly, high embankments were constructed in the 1870s. Despite having had its excesses tamed, the Tiber has not lost any of its magic, and a walk along its banks is a treat on a warm evening – perhaps to the Ponte Fabricio, one of the oldest bridges in the city. This leads to the Isola Tiberina, an island lying in the river opposite what was once the old port of Ostia. After an epidemic in 291 BC, a temple was erected on the island, dedicated to Aesculapius, the god of healing. The church of San Bartolomeo was built on the ruins of this pagan temple in the 10th century.

Street scenes in Trastevere (images, below left). Santa Maria (below right) is said to be the oldest Christian building in Rome. Originally founded in the 3rd century, the façade was restored by Italian baroque architect Carlo Fontana at the turn of the 18th century. Right and middle: The popular Sunday flea market at the Porta Portese; far right: an instrument maker on Vicolo del Cedre.

THE "OTHER" ROME

For Romans born on the right bank of the Tiber, visiting the Trastevere quarter – which literally translates as "across the Tiber" – is almost like going abroad. But naturally, the inhabitants of this area, which was settled at a later date (around 500 BC, though in Rome the term is relative), are proud to live here: they don't see themselves as Romans but rather as "Trasteverini". The layout of the streets also demonstrates that they have maintained a certain independence from the rest of the city; visitors to the area can only find their way around the picturesque labyrinth of narrow alleyways by following the high bell towers of the Romanesque churches. With washing lines often strung high up across the streets between buildings, the cliché of a poor but tightly knit Italian city community is not entirely accurate: in the 1970s the Trastevere area became fashionable, and therefore more expensive. Many of the artisans, students, and artists who had previously found cheap accommodation here were driven out – often after lengthy battles with developers. But not all of the small traditional osterie and little stores have given way to chic bars and boutiques. You may have to search for the original Trastevere today, but you can still find it if you look, somewhere hidden away in the confusion of alleyways.

Memorials to Garibaldi's followers at the historic battle of Rome, on the Gianicolo Hill (below left); Bernini designed the Cappella Raimondi in the church of San Pietro in Montorio (below right). Right: View from Gianicolo over the city at night.

Gianicolo

Named after the Roman god Janus, Gianicolo (the Janiculum Hill) lies on the west bank of the Tiber. The Aurelian Wall was extended up the hill to keep the water mills on the Gianicolo, which were used to grind corn, within the confines of the city. Despite not being one of the classic seven hills of Rome, it has witnessed its share of significant historical events. In 1849, the national hero Giuseppe Garibaldi barricaded himself here against French troops, who crushed the short-lived Roman republic. Memorials to these conflicts, which were precursors to the unification of Italy, show Garibaldi on horseback, looking toward the Vatican, and his wife Anita, also on horseback, a baby in one hand and a gun in the other. These monuments are in marked contrast to their idyllic, leafy surroundings. The hill is much loved by locals and offers superb views over the city.

Below: *The Nymph Callisto on Jupiter's Chariot*, ceiling fresco (1511) by Baldassare Peruzzi in the Sala di Galatea. Peruzzi created a cycle of constellations intended to represent the position of the stars at the time of the birth of Chigi, who commissioned the work. Right: Peruzzi's illusory paintings (1516) in the Hall of Perspective give the impression that the walls are transparent. The courtesan Imperia, Chigi's mistress, is supposed to have been the model for the Grace to the left in Raphael's fresco *Amor Shows Psyche to the Graces* (1518) in the Loggia of Psyche (far right).

VILLA FARNESINA — POMP AND CEREMONY

Completed in 1511, this villa was commissioned by Agostino Chigi (1465–1520) as an idyllic refuge, far from the city which even in those days was filled with bustle and noise. Born in Siena, Chigi, one of the most influential bankers of his time, conducted the affairs of his trading and financial empire from Rome. In 1508 he

called the architect and painter Baldassare Peruzzi from his home town to Rome to design a villa for him. Peruzzi created a building whose exterior was as captivatingly simple as the interior was lavishly decorated. Chigi was also a great patron of the arts, giving commissions to several of the greatest painters of the time, and a

particular friendship was forged with Raphael, from Urbino, to whom he gave his support at every opportunity. Both are said to have been equally fond of celebrating, and the villa was the scene of numerous exuberant parties, at some of which even the pope, Leo X, was present. Among other works, the artist created a cycle of paint-

ings showing Amor and Psyche for his patron's villa, and he is said to have given one of the three Graces depicted in the paintings the features of the famous Roman courtesan Imperia – Chigi's mistress. In 1580, the villa was acquired by Cardinal Alessandro Farnese, whose name it bears today.

According to legend, the basilica of Santa Sabina (below left) was founded in AD 425 on the site of a house belonging to Sabina, a rich Roman woman who converted to Christianity. Below right: A fountain head in the inner courtyard of Santa Sabina. Right: Pines make the Aventine Hill a green oasis.

The Aventine Hill

The Aventine is the southernmost of the seven hills of Rome: its western slope runs down to the Tiber, from where there's a wonderful view of the Isola Tiberina and the Vatican across the river. At the top of the hill, crowned by the 5th-century basilica of Santa Sabina, the hectic life of the city seems far away, which is why it is one of the most popular residential areas in Rome. The Aventine Hill was initially occupied by merchants, who carried out their business on the quays along the Tiber; then the area became chic and the rich and famous built villas here. Emperor Hadrian lived on the Aventine before he became the ruler of the Roman Empire. Between the Aventine and Testaccio is the Protestant cemetery, where many members of the foreign community were buried after dying in Italy – including English Romantic poets John Keats and Percy Bysshe Shelley, who drowned off Livorno.

Modern graffiti on the old walls of Ex Mattatoio in Testaccio (below left), the lively, traditional area beneath the artificial hill of the same name. The slaughterhouse opened in 1891 is today home to the city's experimental artists; concerts are held here, as are craft and food markets. Right: Food sellers in Testaccio.

Testaccio

Monte Testaccio, around 35 m (114 feet) high and located in the district of the same name, is actually an artificial mound almost entirely composed of the broken remains of amphorae (*testae* in Latin) accumulated over the centuries. Amphorae were large clay pots used to store and transport food and wine from the nearby former Tiber port. In the 19th century, the hill was a place of pilgrimage, and its summit is still crowned by a cross. Monte Testaccio is now officially barred to visitors, as amateur archeologists found the opportunity to take a fragment or two home far too tempting. In the 19th century, Testaccio was a residential area for workers at the gas works and the slaughterhouse. Since then, the area has become a trendy meeting place with restaurants, bars, discos, and cultural events. Many of these take place in the former slaughterhouse, Ex Mattatoio, at the foot of the hill.

Below: Designated as Rome's municipal cemetery, the vast Campo Verano is worth a visit for its elaborate tombs, mausoleums, and monuments.
Right: The chancel and cloisters of San Lorenzo fuori le Mura. After St Laurence was tortured to death and buried here, his tomb became a place of pilgrimage.

San Lorenzo fuori le Mura, Campo Verano

The district of San Lorenzo, just outside Rome's eastern walls, suffered serious bomb damage during World War II. The basilica of the same name – dedicated to St Laurence, who died a martyr's death in 258 – was also damaged, but has been restored. It was founded during the reign of the emperor Constantine (4th century), but has been altered and extended many times since then. Today's San Lorenzo fuori le Mura was formed when the existing St Laurence church was joined with an adjacent church dedicated to the Virgin Mary. The relics of St Laurence and other saints are held here and the church also houses the sarcophagus of Pius IX, who died in 1878. Often regarded as the first modern pope, he was the last ruler of the independent Papal States. Founded at the beginning of the 19th century, the adjacent Campo Verano cemetery is the largest in Rome.

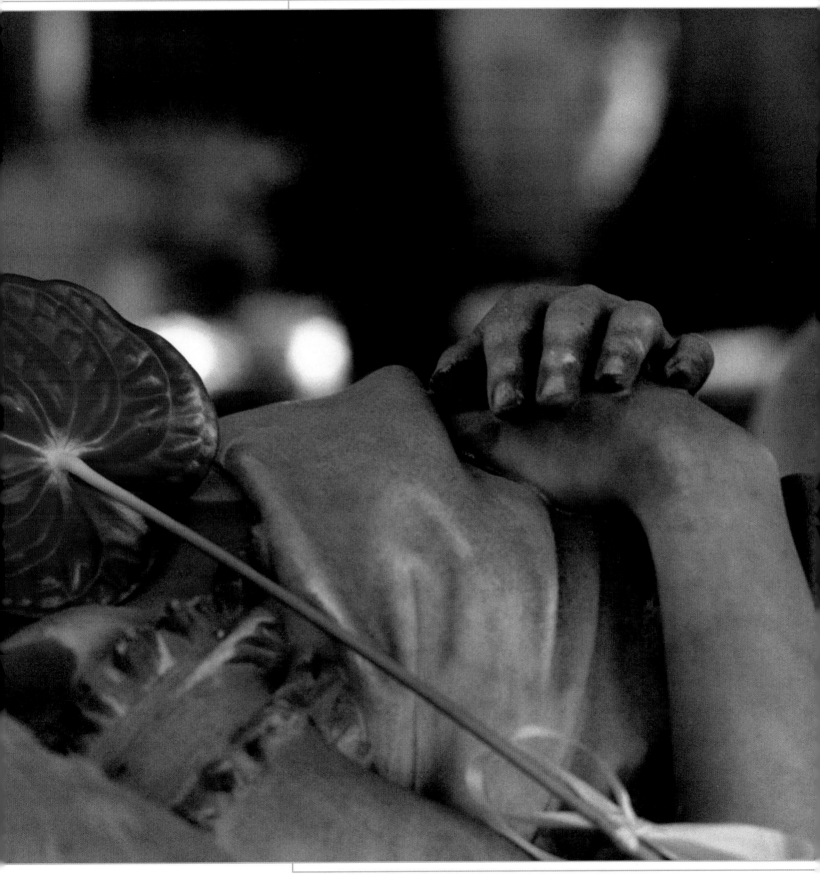

The ceiling in the entrance hall of the Villa Borghese (below left). Bernini's *David* (below, center) and (below right, from top) *Pluto and Proserpina*, Canova's *Paolina Borghese*, and *Sleeping Hermaphrodite*, a Roman copy of a Greek sculpture. Right: Caryatids and Etruscan treasures in the Villa Giulia.

Villa Borghese, Villa Giulia

These two villas on the northern edge of the city are really worth seeing, not just for their architectural beauty but also for their spectacular art collections. Villa Giulia, built between 1551 and 1553 and used by Pope Julius III as a summer palace, once housed the pope's sculpture collection; in 1555 it was removed to the Vatican, filling 160 boats. Today it is the home of a world-class Etruscan Museum. The Villa Borghese, built between 1613 and 1616, was once owned by Cardinal Scipione Borghese, an important patron of the arts. Many statues created for him by Bernini are on display here, together with world-famous works by other artists – such as Titian's *Sacred and Profane Love*. The villas are set in sumptuous gardens, landscaped in the naturalistic English manner, and a work of art in themselves. There is a also a small zoo housing many endangered species.

Mussolini's *urbs magna*, a fascist megalopolis, was supposed to recall the ancient Roman Empire. The most striking structure is the Palazzo della Civiltà del Lavoro, known as "the square Colosseum" by locals (below). The palazzo is faced with travertine marble; statues represent the arts and different trades (right).

EUR

In an exercise to display the glory of fascism, Mussolini planned a World Exhibition for 1942, set in the southern part of Rome, with residential areas, museums, and parks. World War II intervened, and although the Esposizione Universale di Roma (EUR), the Universal Rome Exhibition, never materialized, by 1938 construction was already well underway. Inevitably, as with many projects pursued by Mussolini, existing buildings made way for the new.

The most notable building in the EUR – today a popular residential and business area – is the Palazzo della Civiltà del Lavoro, nicknamed "the square Colosseum". It is proof of Mussolini's desire to link his state with the great ancient Roman Empire. The complex now contains a large sports arena, the Pala Lottomatica, built for the 1960 Summer Olympics, the National Museum of Prehistory and Ethnography, and the Museum of Roman Civilization.

Legendary passion: Marcello Mastroianni and Anita Ekberg in *La Dolce Vita* (below). It was the first film Mastroianni made with Fellini. Subsequently, he became a kind of dramatic alter ego for the director. Right: Film stars Giulietta Masina, Anna Magnani, and Sophia Loren; and the director and actor Roberto Benigni.

FEDERICO FELLINI

DISTRIBUZIONE
CINERIZ

MARCELLO MAST

CINECITTÀ – THE ROMAN DREAM FACTORY

Some 20 km (12 miles) south of the city lies the famous Cinecittà film studio complex, built on the orders of Mussolini in 1937. It covers some 600,000 sq m (717,600 sq yards). Vast water tanks enable film production companies to recreate sea battles – just as the ancient Romans did when they flooded the Colosseum and the Piazza Navona, creating artificial lakes for the same purpose. In 1997, Cinecittà was privatized by the Italian government, and today is owned by a holding company. Legendary films shot here include Federico Fellini's *La Dolce Vita* (1960), starring Marcello Mastroianni and Anita Ekberg, about the dark side of Roman high society, the meaning of life – and love. In Fellini's *Roma* (1972), the city itself is the subject, with Anna Magnani, a native Roman, playing her last role. The 1950s saw the production of the epic *Ben Hur* with its famous chariot race, while more recently Martin Scorsese's *The Gangs of New York* was shot here, as was Mel Gibson's controversial *The Passion of Christ*. The studios are also used by international TV companies such as the BBC and HBO. In 2007 a fire destroyed parts of the studios, but was contained by Italian firefighters who worked through the night. They managed to save the oldest parts, where classics such as *Ben Hur* and many of Fellini's most notable films were made.

On the beach at Ostia: The Romans wanted to control the Tiber as far as the saltworks at the mouth of the river, and a colony was soon established at Ostia (Latin: *ostium*, mouth of a river).

In the Teatro Marittimo of Hadrian's Villa, situated to the west of Tivoli and once a private retreat of Emperor Hadrian, a circular portico frames a huge water basin with a small central island.

BEYOND ROME TO THE SEA

Even in ancient times, the Romans felt the need, particularly in summer, to escape from the city. Those who could afford it bought themselves a villa in the country, where they could relax and recoup their energies – Cicero's estate at Tusculum was famous. These days, there is an exodus from the city on public holidays: the inhabitants of the Italian capital are doubly privileged in that they have the sea on their doorstep to one side and the open countryside, the *campagna*, and the mountains on the other.

Romans flocked to the fashionable Lido di Ostia to escape the oppressive summer heat of the city in the 1950s and 1960s. Its nightclubs were full of the smart set and film stars but its charm eventually faded and the visitor numbers declined. However, Ostia is now becoming chic again and *La dolce vita* has returned.

Ostia

Ostia Antica, the trading and naval port of ancient Rome, was built in the 4th and 3rd centuries BC around 25 km (15 miles) south of Rome. Originally situated on the coast at the mouth of the Tiber, the site is now 3 km (2 miles) inland due to the silting up of the area. Excavations revealed that the city flourished for many centuries with magnificent houses, markets, public baths, taverns, sports complexes, and a playhouse – many of its buildings have been well preserved and can still be seen today. The gradual silting up of the port contributed to its decline and it was abandoned in the 9th century. Work began on reclaiming coastal land in 1883 and modern Ostia (also known as Lido de Roma) was founded in 1908. Mussolini ensured Rome could easily access its new suburb by building a new road and there is also a rail link, the journey taking around 30 minutes.

Tivoli is famous for its two UNESCO World Heritage Sites: Hadrian's Villa (far right and below, far right), AD 117–134, is a perfect example of Roman elegance and opulence; the Renaissaince Villa d'Este (all other images) is noted for its spectacular gardens, with elaborate water cascades, fountains, and pools.

Tivoli

Tivoli has been Rome's summer resort for over 2,000 years. Thanks to its position in the Monti Tiburtini, some 30 km (19 miles) from the city, the air here has always been fresh and there are mineral-rich healing springs. Finding it much easier to sleep in Tivoli, the emperor Augustus had a villa built here, while Hadrian's Villa Adriana is located 6 km (4 miles) to the south. It includes a pool lined with columns and an artificial grotto, a refuge where the emperor could pursue his love of painting. In the Renaissance era, with the renewed interest in ancient times, the resort underwent a revival. One of the most impressive palaces from this period is the Villa d'Este, famed for its terraced gardens, while the Villa Gregoriana is located in a deep valley through which the Aniene River courses down in spectacular fashion, culminating in the Grande Cascata waterfall, which falls 108 m (356 feet).

Trading with the Greeks brought the Etruscans Corinthian ceramics and vases with painted black figures, and these influenced the Etruscans' own creations. Popular motifs included everyday scenes (below: a slave prepares a meal for a Symposium) as well as mythological figures. Right: The sarcophagus of an Etruscan married couple; the banquet of Eurythio and Hercules (all illustrations are of finds from the Cerveteri necropolis).

THE ETRUSCANS – VIVACITY AND PIETY

Few of the great ancient cultures shone so brightly and were extinguished so quickly as the Etruscans. Of disputed ancestry and originating from a relatively small area lying between the Arno and the Tiber on the Tyrrhenian side of the Italian peninsula, the Etruscans spread so quickly that the Roman historian Livy reported that at the height of its power, Etruria filled "all Italy, from the Alps to the Straits of Messina, with the glory of its name". The Etruscans formed city states which were ruled by kings until the end of the 6th century BC, and then by elected officials from the 5th century BC, in a loose confederation comprising twelve states. The rise of Rome sealed their fate, and this great culture was soon completely lost to the fog of history. Although the Etruscans had a fatalistic notion of the role of divine power in shaping human fates, their culture displayed a very vigorous celebration of life. They created one of the most advanced civilizations in the Western world, bequeathing writing and the alphabet to the Romans, although no great literary works in the Etruscan language have ever been discovered. Significant finds of Etruscan culture have been made at Cerveteri and Tarquinia, Volterra, Arezzo, Perugia, Cortona, Chiusi, Populonia, Rusellae, Vulci, Veji, and Volsinii (Orvieto).

The Greek influence on Etruscan culture can mainly be seen in their sculpture. Right: Greek vase from Cerveteri and Etruscan sculptures. Below: Sarcophagi in the National Museum in the Palazzo Vitelleschi in the medieval town of Tarquinia, and a dancer from the "Priest's Tomb" in Tarquinia.

Cerveteri and Tarquinia

Situated in the modern provinces of Rome and Viterbo, the towns of Cerveteri and Tarquinia are famous for their superb Etruscan necropolises, for which they have been jointly declared a World Heritage Site. The tombs, which show the different burial practices of the northern Mediterranean's earliest civilizations, depict the everyday lives of the people who lived here. Cerveteri is famous for the architecture and sculpture of its tombs, with a variety of forms – some carved from rock and topped with burial mounds, with corridors and rooms that give an idea of Etruscan home life and decor. Other square-shaped tombs are laid out in streets with small courtyards like a small town. The tombs at Tarquinia are best known for their frescoes depicting banquets, dancing, and hunting scenes. Many of the 6,000 tombs are yet to be excavated – so far some 200 painted tombs have been found.

Fountains and water features decorate the gardens of the Villa Aldobrandini in Frascati (below left and right). Right: Villa Aldobrandini in Frascati; Observatory and the papal palace at Castel Gandolfo, the pope's summer residence.

Castel Gandolfo, Frascati

Castel Gandolfo is a small town on the edge of a crater lake in the Colli Albani (Alban Hills), on the site of the ancient city of Alba Longa, founded some time after 1150 BC and destroyed by the Romans. Castel Gandolfo is best known for being the papal summer residence – even the pope has to have his house in the country. The Catholic Church purchased the castello toward the end of the 16th century and in 1628 Pope Urban VIII had a villa constructed on the site by Maderno. The country seat of Emperor Domitian (around AD 90) was also located here. Castel Gandolfo is not open to the public. Frascati, north of Castel Gandolfo, was a holiday resort for the Roman *jeunesse dorée* in ancient times. Today it is known not only for its villas dating from the 16th and 17th centuries – such as Villa Aldobrandini – but also for the crisp white wine that is cultivated in the area.

Simple *joie de vivre:* if the city has something to celebrate, such as here, the Italian victory in the 2006 football World Cup, jubilant crowds soon assemble on the streets.

ATLAS

Rome wasn't built in a day, but "can be done in a day", according to the Swedish playwright and writer August Strindberg (1849–1912), who was obviously in a hurry. "I didn't come here to see it, I came here to have seen it" he said, and with that he ticked off the sights in a horse-drawn carriage, finding some things "quite nice", others "very basic", but in general "everything as it ought to be". At the Colosseum he asked "do I have to get out?" and he later summed up the city as "rather grand, but I prefer the photographs".

The Piazza di Spagna has been a popular spot for visitors to Rome for some 300 years. It is also an ideal starting point for walking tours of the city. Begin by taking in the view from the Spanish Steps and then head off to explore the sights.

KEY TO THE MAPS 1 : 15 000

Expressway (primary route)

Arterial (major) road

Other road

Local (side) road

Footpath

Pedestrian zone

Railroad (railway)

Industrial railroad (railway)

Regional/Suburban railroad (railway)

Subway (underground)

Car ferry; Passenger ferry

Densely built-up area; Thinly built-up area

Public building

Building of note; Industrial building

Green space; Cemetery; Wooded area

Jewish cemetery

KEY

The map extracts on the following pages show Rome in 1:15,000 scale (general map 1:315,000). Tourist information is included. The road network is clearly shown and symbols explain the location and nature of important sights such as churches, museums, castles, government buildings, and theaters.

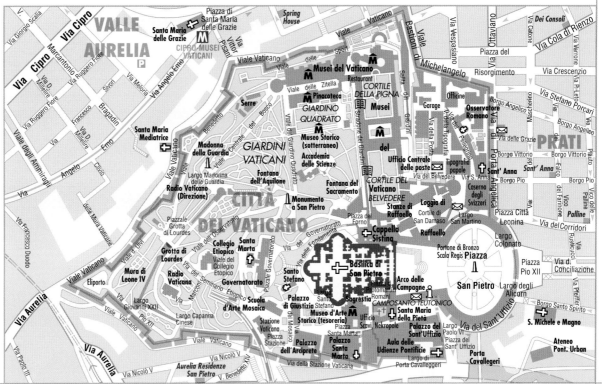

Principal travel routes

Road routes

Remarkable landscapes and natural monuments

Cave
Waterfall/rapids
Botanic gardens

Nature park
Lakeland area
Coastal area

	Kb	Kc	Kd	La	Lb

Tarquínia
Museo nazionale
Tarquinia Vecchia
Poggio del Forno 247

Palazzo Vitelleschi
Necrópoli Etrusca
Monte Romano

Staz. di Tarquinia
Casale Turchina
Casale Santa Maria

118
Tarquinia Lido

Blera
Ponte Etrusco
Ponte Romano
Necrópoli Etrusca
S. Giuliano
Barbarano Romano

Monte Cuoco 560
Poggio di Cóccia 612

Vejano

Capránica
Capránica Scalo
Madonna del Parto
Sutri
Anfiteatro Romano
Parco Urbano Antica Città di Sutri

Cant. Trenta Miglia
Castello Borgia
Nepi

Rid Vicano
Bis. Nat. Mte Soratte
Castél Sant'Elia
Faléria
Calcata
SS. Nome di Gesù

Zona Archeologica San Giovenale
Civitella Cesi

Bassano Romano
Staz. di Bassano Romano
Lago di Monteroso Gabelletta

Monte Calvi 587
Monte Rocca Romana 612
Sette Vene

Terme dei Gracchi
Mazzano Romano
Rignano Flamínio

Riserva Naturale Salina di Tarquinia
Lombardi
Mignone
Cencelle
Casale le Centocelle

Sant'Agostino
Casa Pantano
Torre San Agostino

la Farnesiana
Monte Sassicari 526

Allumiere
Sant'António
Tolfa
Rocca
Bianca
Monte Turco 450

Oriolo Romano
Montevirginio

Monte dell'Olmo
Trevignano Romano
Parco Naturale Regionale di Bracciano-Martignano

Autodromo di Vallelunga
Magliano Romano
Palazzo Municipale
Campagnano di Roma

Poggio le Forche 530
Vicarello
Bagni di Vicarello

Cappuccini
Castél degli Ors
Catelnuo di Po

119
Tombe Etrusche
SCÁGLIA

Monti della Tolfa
Madonna della Rocca
Rota
Monte Ísola 344

Riserva Nat. Monterano
Canale Monterano
Quadroni
San Liberato

Vigna Grande
Lago di Bracciano
Lago di Martignano
376 Mte.S.Angelo
Baccano
Sorbo

Sacrofano
San Giova Battista

Civitavécchia Nord
Terme Taurine
Monte Tolfáccia 579

Monumento Naturale Caldara di Manziana
Bagni di Stigliano
Manziana
Pisciarelli
Roma Flash Sporting
Bagni
Anguillara Sabázia
Museo Nazionale Preistorico Etnografico

Formello
la Villa
247

Statua di Giuseppe Garibaldi
Mte.Paradiso 327
Civitavécchia Sud
14
IC/EC
12
E80

Monte Acqua Tosta 520
Castello Orsini
Bracciano
Mte.S.Vito

Vigna di Vallè
493
l'Immacolata

Stabilimento Acqua Cláudia
Parco Regionale di Veio

Forte Michelangelo
CIVITAVÉCCHIA
Torre Marangone
Villaggio del Fanciullo

Monte Rosso 203
Monte Grande 311

Monte Paparano 392
Castél Giuliano
Sasso 430

Casáccia
OSTERIA NUOVA
OLGIATA
Necrópoli

Capo Linaro
Santa Marinella
Santa Severa

Grottini
Tirreno
24

Monte Santo
Mte.Santo
16
la Ríccia
Casaletto di Sotto

Véio
Ponte Sodo 13
ISOLA FARNESE
ARCO DEL PINO

Pyrgi
21

Tomba Etrusca
Necrópoli della Banditaccia

Galéria
SANTA MARIA DI GALERIA
Casale Centrone
LA STORTA
IL PINO
SPIZZICHINO
IL CENTRO
LA GIUSTINIANA

120
Riserva Naturale Macchiatonda
Cerenova
Campo di Mare

CERVÉTERI
Cervéteri Ladispoli
Monumento ai caduti
12
Ceri
Borgo Vaccina

Tragliatella
Tragliata

BOCCEA

Seven Hills Camping
Selva Candida
SELVA CANDIDA LUCCHINA
OTTÁVIA
SANT' ONOFRIO
TOMBA DI NERONE
ss2 Cassia

Torre di Flávia
Castellaccio dei Monteroni

Castello Odescalchi
15
Álsium
Palo

Casale di Castèl Campanile
28
Torrimpietra
Stádio Olimpico
TORREVÉCCHIA
PRIMAVALLE

Ladíspoli
Giard. d. Orchidee del Mediterraneo
Ruderi di San Nicola
Marina di Palidoro
Passo Oscuro

Castèl la Bottáccia di Guido
la Selce
Lorium
la Monachina

Pantan Monastero
BORGATA CASOLOTTI
MONTE SPACCATO
CITTÀ DEL VATICANO
San Pietro

121
FREGENE

Ponte Tre Denari
Bonifica delle Pagliete
Riserva Naturale
Arrone
Maccarese-Fregene
ss1 Aurelia
Terme di Carac

Maccarese
Torre Maccarese
Litorale Romano
Castèl Malnome
ROMA
GIANICOLENS

V.d.Pescaccio
la Pisana
la Pisana
CORVIALE
San Tuori

Bonifica di Maccarese
Ponte Galéria
12
Casa Mattei
Magliana
Magliana
7
6

Focene
Aeroporto Intercontinentale Roma-Fiumicino (Leonardo da Vinci)
91
5
Bonifica di Porto
Fiume Tévere
Ponte Galéria
E80
ss8 Via del Mare/Ostiense
ss8 Via
6
6
E.U.R.
MOSTACCIANO

FIUMICINO
Fiumicino
Parco Torlonia
VILLÁGGIO SAN FRANCESCO
ACILIA
Via Cristóforo Colombo
Ponti

122
Necrópoli
ISOLA SACRA
Ostia Antica
Castèl Fusano
CASAL BERNOCCHI
TOR DE CENCI
CASAL PALOCCO
SP INACETO
Castèl Porziano
INFERNETTO
SELCE
CASTÉL DI DECIM

Lido del Faro
Parco Urbano di Castèl Fusano
Tenuta di Cáccia
Riserva

Mar
LIDO DI ÓSTIA
Camping Internazionale di Castel Fusano
CASTÉL FUSANO
LIDO DI
Villa di Plínio Laurentum
601
Cascina Capocotta

Tirreno

Tor Paterno
17
PRÁTICA
Lavin

123
Guardapasso
Zingarini
Tor Vaiánica

	Kb	Kc	Kd	La	Lb

The index entries refer to both the maps and the illustrated section. Page numbers printed in bold and map square references printed directly after each entry refer to the map section. Page references printed after this refer to the illustrated section, and the last entry provides web links enabling easy access to further information about the sights described in this book. The majority of the references in the illustrated section can also be found in the map section, which also provides a wide range of tourist information.

This city is loved "like a being with a soul, its buildings, its ruins, are friends, to whom one says farewell" (Madame de Staël). From left: Via Appia Antica, the Colosseum, the Arch of Constantine, St Peter's Square.

From left: Bernini's allegorical Fountain of the Four Rivers and the Fontana del Moro on the Piazza Navona; Fontana della Barcaccia by the Spanish Steps; on the Tiber; across the rooftops of Trastevere; on the Piazza della Rotonda.

Picture Credits

Abbreviations:

A   Alamy
B   The Bridgeman Art Library
C   Corbis
FMF   Franz Marc Frei
G   Getty Images
L   Laif
UB   Udo Bernhart

Picture credits are given per page, from top left to below right.

Front cover: (top) Premium, M. Getty, (bottom) ifa/Alastor Photo; Spine: akg-images/Mimatallah; Back cover: Premium/Pan. Images/Cajko

Page: 1 L/hemis; 2/3 Bilderberg/Keystone, 4/5 Premium, 6/7 Freyer, 8 Freyer, 8/9 Freyer, 10.1 akg/Lessing, 10.2 akg/Pirozzi, 10.3 akg, 10/11 (top) Bilderberg/T. Ernsting, 10/11 (bottom) akg, 11.1 akg, 11.2 akg/Electa, 12.1 akg, 12.2 A/Visual Arts Library, 12.3 B/British Museum, 12.4 C/The Art Archiv, 13.1 akg, 13.2 akg/Lessing, 13.3 akg/Lessing, 13.4 C/Archivo Iconografico, 13.5 A/Widmann, 14.1 akg/Lessing, 14.2 B/Alinari, 14.3 akg, 14.4 B, 14.5 akg/CDA/Guillemot, 14/15 akg/Lessing, 15.1 B/Index, 15.2 B/Alinari, 15.3 akg/Nimatallah, 16.1 akg, 16.2 B/Index, 16.3 C/A. de Luca, 16.4 akg/Nimatallah, 16.5 akg/Connolly, 16.6 akg/Connolly, 16.7 akg/Connolly, 16/17 FMF, 17.1 akg/Lessing, 17.2 akg/Lessing, 17.3 akg/Pirozzi, 17.4 G/National Geographic/Mazzatenta, 18.1 C/Bettmann, 18.2 C/The Art Archiv, 18.3 C/Hulton-Deutsch Collection, 18.4 UB, 18.5 akg/Jemolo, 18/19 Freyer, 19 akg/ Lafranchis, 20.1 C/A. de Luca, 20.2 akg/Jemolo, 20.3 akg/Rabatti – Domingie, 20/21 A/JLImages, 21.1 UB, 21.2 akg/Lessing, 21.3 akg/Lessing, 21.4 L/Caccuri, 21.5

L/Caccuri, 22.1 C/A. de Luca, 22.2 akg, 22.3 akg, 22.4 B, 22.5 akg, 22.6 akg, 23.1 Freyer, 23.2 B/Bonhams, 23.3 C/A. de Luca, 23.4 C/Immaginazione/Osservatore Romano, 24.1 akg, 24.2 akg, 24.3 akg/Cameraphoto, 24.4 akg, 24.5 C/Jose Fuste Raga, 24.6 L/hemis, 25.1 akg/Lessing, 25.2 akg, 25.3 A/AEP, 25.4 akg/Electa, 26.1 C Sygma/Cevallus, 26.2 C/Bettmann, 26.3 G/AFP, 26.4 akg/Excelsa/Mayer-Burstyn/Album/A, 26.5 A/Connett, 26.6 A/Rough Guides, 27.1 G, 27.2 G/AFP, 27.3 C/epa/Schmidt, 27.4 L/Contrasto/Lanzilao, 27.5 A/Segre, 27.6 L/Contrasto/Lanzilao, 27.7 L/Contrasto/Lanzilao, 27.8 L/Contrasto/Lanzilao, 28 L/Galli, 28/29 A/CuboImages srl, 30.1 A/Wilmar Photography, 30.2 A/Wilmar Photography, 30.3 A/Wilmar Photography, 30/31 L/Galli, 32.1 akg/Lafranchis, 32.2 akg/Lafranchis, 32.3 A/G. W. Williams, 32/33 A/Premium GPics, 34.1 L/Galli, 34.2 L/Galli, 34.3 L/Galli, 34/35 L/Martini, 35 G/Simeone Huber, 36.1 L/Hemis, 36.2 L/Hemis, 36.3 A/Sims, 36.4 A/Sims, 36.5 A/Sims, 36.6 L/Celentano, 36/37 L/Hemis, 37 L/Hemis, 38 Bilderberg/Ernsting, 38/39 L/Zanettini, 39 Schapowalow/SIME, 40.1 akg/Electa, 40.2 akg/Lessing, 40/41 akg/Jemolo, 42.1 akg/Lessing, 42.2 C/A. de Luca, 42/43 A/Rough Guides, 44.1 C/Atlantide Phototravel, 44.2 C/Atlantide Phototravel, 44/45 A/Art Kowalsky, 45 A/mcx images, 46.1 L/Zanettini, 46.2 L/hemis, 46/47 L/Galli, 47 L/hemis, 48.1 A/Werner Otto, 48.2 C/A.o de Luca, 48.3 L/Kristensen, 48.4 C/Tweedy-Holmes, 48/49 L/hemis, 49.1 L/Galli, 49.2 G/S. Otte, 49.3 L/Zanettini, 50.1 L/hemis/R. Mattes, 50.2 L/hemis/E. Suettone, 50.3 A/E. Gerald, 50.4 L/hemis/S. Frances, 50.5 L/hemis/S. Frances, 51.1 A/cuboImages srl, 51.2 A/E. Gerald, 51.3 A/K. deWitt, 51.4 A/E. Gerald, 51.5 A/M. Spironetti, 51.6 G/The Image Bank/Krecichwost, 51.7 L/Galli, 51.8 L/The NewYork-Times/Redux, 51.9 A/M. Juno, 51.10 Look/H. Dressler, 52.1 A/N. Asuni, 52.2 G/Photogra-

phers Choice/S. Huber, 52.3 G/Photographers Choice/U. Sjostedt, 52.4 A/J. Tack, 52/53 ifa, 54 A/Photodisc, 54/55 L/hemis, 56 Cajho Panorama Images, 56/57 L/hemis/R. Mattes, 58.1 L/hemis/R. Mattes, 58.2 vision Photos, 58/59 L/hemis/R. Mattes, 60.1 akg/Pirozzi, 60.2 Mauritius/R. Mattes, 60/61 Visum/G. Westrich, 61 C/D. Lees, 62.1 L/Galli, 62.2 A/E. Gerald, 62/63 L/hemis/R. Mattes, 64.1 C/V. Rastelli, 64.2 C/A. de Luca, 64.3 C/V. Rastelli, 64.4 C/V. Rastelli, 64/65 L/Celentano, 66 A/Reimar, 66/67 akg/W. Forman, 67 akg/W. Forman, 68.1 Bilderberg/Ellerbrock & Schafft, 68.2 L/hemis/B. Gardel, 68/69 FMF, 70.1 FMF, 70.2 L/Celentano, 70/71 L/hemis/R. Mattes, 72 A/E. Gerald, 72/73 L/Galli, 74 A/G. W. Williams, 74/75 A/imagebroker, 76 Bildarchiv Monheim/A. Bednorz, 76/77 FMF, 78 A/The Print Collector, 78/79 A/Lordprice Collection, 79.1 akg/Sotheby's, 79.2 akg, 80.1 A/N. Walstow, 80.2 A, 80.3 C/A. de Luca, 80/81 Bildagentur Huber, 81 B/Index, 82.1 A/aep, 82.2 A/A. Eastland, 82/83 A/G. Thomas, 84 ifa, 84/85 L/Bialobrzeski, 86 G/Altrendo Images, 86/87 G/travelpix Ltd., 88.1 akg, 88.2 akg, 88.3 akg, 88.4 akg, 88.5 akg, 88.6 akg, 88.7 C/Reuters, 88/89 L/Contrasto, 89 L/Contrasto, 90 ifa/Alastor Photo, 90/91 Bildagentur Huber/Simeone, 92 akg, 92/93 akg, 93 akg, 94.1 A/ArkReligion.com, 94.2 L/Galli, 94.3 L/Galli, 94/95 L/Galli, 96 akg, 96/97 UB, 97 C/Pizzoli, 98.1 A/P. Barritt, 98.2 akg, 98/99 L/Galli, 100.1 L/Galli, 100.2 L/Galli, 100.3 A/P. Horree, 100/101 A/Robert Harding Picture Library Ltd., 101 B, 102 akg, 102/103 akg, 103 akg, 104.1 Look/travelstock44, 104.2 G/S. Otte, 104.3 L/Celentano, 104.4 G/D. C. Tomlinson, 104.5 Bildagentur Huber/Bernhart, 104/105 G/J. Walker, 106.1 C/dpa/L. Halbauer, 106.2 A/CuboImages srl, 106/107 C/Alinari Archives, 107 A/AM Corporation, 108 G/The Image Bank/A. Pistolesi, 108/109 R. Freyer, 110 Bildagentur

Huber/Bernhart, 110/111 L/Polaris, 111 Schapowalow/SIME, 112 L/Galli, 112/113 FMF, 114.1 L/hemis/R. Mattes, 114.2 FMF, 114.3 A/E. Gerald, 114.4 L/hemis/R. Mattes, 114.5 L/hemis/R. Mattes, 114/115 FMF, 116.1 C/Reuters/A. Bianchi, 116.2 C/Reuters/T. Gentile, 116/117 L/Galli, 118.1 FMF, 118.2 FMF, 118.3 L/Gonzalez, 118.4 FMF, 118.5 A/E. Gerald, 118/119 L/Gonzalez, 120 L/Celentano, 120/121 A/J. Tack, 121 A/A. Eastland, 122.1 akg, 122.2 akg, 122/123 akg, 124 R. Freyer, 124/125 A/Bildarchiv Monheim, 125 FMF, 126.1 L/E. Vandeville, 126.2 A/A. Eastland, 126.3 Look/Lubenow, 126/127 A/Rough Guides, 127 A/N. Robinson, 128.1 A/A. Matone, 128.2 A/AEP, 128/129 A/J. Ferro Sims, 130.1 C/M. Listri, 130.2 A/P. Horree, 130.3 A/P. Horree, 130/131 L/E. Scorcelletti, 131.1 L/hemis/M. Borgese, 131.2 L/hemis/M. Borgese, 131.3 L/Keystone-France/Faillet, 131.4 C/M. Listri, 132.1 A/CuboImages srl, 132.2 G/O. Olivieri, 1332/133 L/Galli, 134.1 A/Photos 12, 134.2 A/Photos 12, 134.3 A/Pictorial Press Ltd, 134.4 C/N. Guerin, 134.5 G, 134/135 A/Pictorial Press Ltd, 135 G, 136 G/T. Macpherson, 136/137 G/AFP, 138.1 L/Contrasto, 138.2 L/Contrasto, 138/139 L/Zuder, 140.1 G/Photographer's Choice/S. Bergman, 140.2 C/A. de Luca, 140.3 Bilderberg/F. Blickle, 140.4 G/Bridgeman Art Library/Italian School, 140.5 L/hemis/R. Mattes, 141.1 Bildagentur-online/Lescourret, 141.2 Focus, 142.1 C/A. de Luca, 142.2 B, 142/143 B, 144.1 C/A. de Luca, 144.2 C/A. de Luca, 144.3 C/The Art Archive, 144/145 G/National Geographic, 145 B, 146.1 Schapowalow/SIME, 146.2 C/Reuters/T. Gentile, 146.3 L/E. Vandeville, 146/ 147 Schapowalow/SIME, 147 Bildarchiv Monheim/F. Monheim, 148/149 A, 150/151 G.

MONACO BOOKS is an imprint of Verlag Wolfgang Kunth
© Verlag Wolfgang Kunth GmbH & Co.KG, Munich, 2009

© Cartography: GeoGraphic Publishers GmbH & Co. KG
Representation of terrain MHM ® Copyright © Digital Wisdom, Inc.

Text: Michael Müller
English translation: JMS Books LLP (translation: Nicola Coates, Malcolm Garrard; editor: Maggie Ramsay, Jenni Davis; design: cbdesign)

For distribution please contact:
Monaco Books
c/o Verlag Wolfgang Kunth, Königinstr. 11
80539 München, Germany
Tel: +49 / 89/45 80 20 23
Fax: +49 / 89/ 45 80 20 21
info@kunth-verlag.de
www.monacobooks.com
www.kunth-verlag.de

Printed in Slovakia